The Most Important Questions to Ask on Your Next Job Interview

Insider Secrets You Need to Know

By Kendall Blair

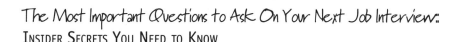

The Most Important Questions to Ask On Your Next Job Interview:
INSIDER SECRETS YOU NEED TO KNOW

Copyright © 2007 by Atlantic Publishing Group, Inc.
1405 SW 6th Ave. • Ocala, Florida 34471 • 800-814-1132 • 352-622-1875–Fax
Web site: www.atlantic-pub.com • E-mail: sales@atlantic-pub.com
SAN Number: 268-1250

ISBN-13: 978-1-60138-133-0   ISBN-10: 1-60138-133-6

Blair, Kendall, 1983-
  The most important questions to ask on your next job interview : insider secrets you need to know / Kendall Blair.
      p. cm.
  Includes bibliographical references and index.
  ISBN-13: 978-1-60138-133-0 (alk. paper)
  ISBN-10: 1-60138-133-6 (alk. paper)
  1. Employment interviewing. 2. Job hunting. 3. Corporate culture. 4. Work environment. 5. Personality and occupation. I. Title. II. Title: Questions to ask on your next job interview.

  HF5549.5.I6B555 2008
  650.14'4--dc22
                         2008005490

INTERIOR LAYOUT DESIGN: Vickie Taylor • vtaylor@atlantic-pub.com

Printed in the United States

Printed on Recycled Paper

Dedication

This book is dedicated to my husband, William Blair. William is an amazing individual who puts up with all of my constant changing. He is an extremely intelligent and loving person, and I am extremely blessed to have him as my number one. He is my "left brain." When he is not helping me with this or that, he is encouraging me and pushing me forward. William keeps me on my toes. He is always great for a laugh, and he is even better for a hug.

I am extremely blessed to have him in my life. He makes each day something to look forward to. All of our experiences together never seem to gather dust. It is amazing to have someone and something so incredibly concrete. My love for him has never been questioned. He is my rock - the answer to many prayers. Without him, I would have never had the courage to take on the task of writing this book, or the courage to go through the interviews that brought me all of this knowledge.

Will is an amazing man, husband, and friend.

We recently lost our beloved pet "Bear," who was not only our best and dearest friend but also the "Vice President of Sunshine" here at Atlantic Publishing. He did not receive a salary but worked tirelessly 24 hours a day to please his parents. Bear was a rescue dog that turned around and showered myself, my wife Sherri, his grandparents Jean, Bob and Nancy and every person and animal he met (maybe not rabbits) with friendship and love. He made a lot of people smile every day.

We wanted you to know that a portion of the profits of this book will be donated to The Humane Society of the United States. *–Douglas & Sherri Brown*

The human-animal bond is as old as human history. We cherish our animal companions for their unconditional affection and acceptance. We feel a thrill when we glimpse wild creatures in their natural habitat or in our own backyard.

Unfortunately, the human-animal bond has at times been weakened. Humans have exploited some animal species to the point of extinction.

The Humane Society of the United States makes a difference in the lives of animals here at home and worldwide. The HSUS is dedicated to creating a world where our relationship with animals is guided by compassion. We seek a truly humane society in which animals are respected for their intrinsic value, and where the human-animal bond is strong.

Want to help animals? We have plenty of suggestions. Adopt a pet from a local shelter, join The Humane Society and be a part of our work to help companion animals and wildlife. You will be funding our educational, legislative, investigative and outreach projects in the U.S. and across the globe.

Or perhaps you'd like to make a memorial donation in honor of a pet, friend or relative? You can through our Kindred Spirits program. And if you'd like to contribute in a more structured way, our Planned Giving Office has suggestions about estate planning, annuities, and even gifts of stock that avoid capital gains taxes.

Maybe you have land that you would like to preserve as a lasting habitat for wildlife. Our Wildlife Land Trust can help you. Perhaps the land you want to share is a backyard— that's enough. Our Urban Wildlife Sanctuary Program will show you how to create a habitat for your wild neighbors.

So you see, it's easy to help animals. And The HSUS is here to help.

THE HUMANE SOCIETY
OF THE UNITED STATES.

2100 L Street NW • Washington, DC 20037 • 202-452-1100

www.hsus.org

Table of Contents

Introduction

Universally, interviews are dreaded. No amount of preparation is able to eliminate the anxiety that comes with going through the interview process. Although there is the ultimate anxiousness, the interviewees do not have to continually fret. An interview is a two-way street. The person holding the interview should not possess all of the power. It is important to come to the interview equipped with questions and requirements of your own. Being prepared with questions ultimately makes the interview process less of a worry and more of a beneficial conversation that can in turn lead to your success.

Research for this book entailed interviewing ten people from a variety of different places within their careers. These people range from first-year employees to hiring managers in major corporations. All bring great insight into the interviewing process. They each have their own opinions and ways of going about things. They are men and women from all over the United States. Each has had his or her personal experiences within the job market. Their thoughts and opinions are shared throughout this book.

First, meet Craig Fowler, vice president of training and business development at Pinnacle Health Group, Houston,

Texas. When asked the question, "What is the interviewing process like at your place of work?," Fowler answered, "We are a small recruiting and consulting firm, so our interview process is fairly simple, yet thorough. We start with a telephone interview with me, and then I send an electronic 'work-value' questionnaire. Once I score the questionnaire, I will schedule the candidate for a face-to-face interview with me. The second face-to-face interview is with our Ethics, Values, Professionalism (EVP) of recruiting and our Chief Financial Officer (CFO). The final face-to-face is with our Chief Executive Officer (CEO) and Chief Operating Officer (COO). All the parties then collectively decide if we should move forward."

All organizations have a different way of approaching the interview process. Here Fowler is describing the steps that his company goes through. So be certain to ask questions about the process during the initial phone conversation or via e-mail. This way you know the situation you are facing upon your arrival.

There are many things to consider when approaching an interview. Obviously, if you were able to get a scheduled interview you are interested enough in the position to have submitted you résumé. Consider if this is enough. Just because someone is interested in a position does not mean it is right for him or her. The interview process is your tool to better acquaint yourself with the organization, and find out if this is the correct place for you. Keep your eyes and ears peeled. Make note of all of your encounters, and consider everything before making a final decision.

Ultimately, it is imperative to be prepared for the interview.

This is noted in just about every resource connected to interview advice. The way you look (your first impression) should make a statement. You should dress as if you are prepared and confident that you are going to receive the position. Besides appearance, your goal is to "wow" the interviewer. It is important to sound intelligent and to be well qualified for the position for which you are interviewing. You can do this by asking the right questions.

Joseph A. McCormack, founder and managing partner of McCormack & Associates, Los Angeles, is an expert in recruiting and interviewing job candidates. He says that the most important question in a job interview is the one that the candidate asks. During an interview, the interviewer usually turns the tables and has the candidate ask some questions. This is your time to shine and set yourself apart from other qualified applicants.

McCormack recommends not waiting for the interviewer to give you the opportunity to ask questions. He says, "After a candidate has exchanged pleasantries with the interviewer, I would ask, 'Before we begin, please tell me what the most important things are that you need to know about my background or experience for this position so that I can be focused and helpful in my responses to your questions.' This will show the employer that you are willing and able to make the most out of this situation."

Here is a great opportunity for you to learn the specifics about the company. Ask questions pertaining to the work environment. Even if you have a good idea of what types of assignments and tasks will be given to you, have the employer qualify what types of daily tasks you will be tackling. You may also want to have the employer go over the chain of command. Where exactly are you going to stand on this organization's ladder if given the particular position you are interviewing for? This answer leads you to look into your ability to move your way through the ranks in the coming years. Does this company provide room for advancement and progress? These are all questions that should be taken into consideration.

These questions ultimately lead to the answer to the question, "Is this position right for you?" (Chapter Five goes over this in depth). Do all signs point to yes? Or are you feeling uneasy about the position? Being able to decipher why the company chose you to interview increases your ability to lead the interview in the right direction. (See Why Me? - Chapter Eight).

As it is said, people come with "baggage." This is true to both people and companies. All organizations have their problems. It is good to recognize these imperfections going into the interview, and to ask questions that pertain to this particular company's difficulties. This might sound odd, but finding out where a company is weak can tell you a great deal about how and why the organization operates as it does.

Finally, when the end of the interview is nearing you should give the interviewer the opportunity to ask any more questions that he or she might have. Simply ask, "What Have I Left Out" (Chapter Ten). This opens the door to the interviewer. It shows that you are able to answer all the questions he or she might have for you. Asking this question may also eliminate a second or third interview.

Before you leave the interview, you may want to ask the interviewer for guidance. Regardless of how the interview is going you want to leave ahead of the game. Gaining direction here is beneficial. You should not allow this process to be a waste of time. No matter what, you want to at least learn something from the interview. Every experience in life makes us who we are. Moreover who better to ask guidance from then a top executive at the organization, which you admired enough to ask for an interview.

1

Interview Questions

First Impressions

First impressions are extremely important. You want to impress the employer at first glance. Do your research on the company's dress code. Find out in advance if you will be walking into a business-casual environment. A business suit is usually proper attire regardless of the situation. Black is a safe choice. Besides clothing, basic "maintenance" is also necessary. Therefore, go the extra mile and show your manicured self.

Craig Fowler of Pinnacle Health Group said, "Natural confidence. In sales, which recruiting at its core is, everyone is confident. I am looking for an unrehearsed, natural, humble confidence. In addition, I am looking for someone who can speak well, someone who is articulate, someone who is friendly, and they have to be coachable. If the person has these qualities, then we can discuss their sales numbers, accomplishments, work ethic, etc."

If you are not confident with yourself and your skills, this shows. It is always essential to walk into an interview prepared and self-assured. Work on your interview outfit. Go for something that looks professional, and makes you feel good. If you feel you look like a million bucks, then it shows. Another fun trick is to wear your favorite underwear. The employer will not know, but you will, and this will help you exude confidence. Everyone is more confident when he or she looks and feels his or her best.

Small Talk

When walking into a room, no matter if there is one person or ten, you need to shake everyone's hand, and look each person in the eye, introduce yourself assertively. If you have a hard time with names, it is a good idea to say that person's name back to him or her. Here is an example, "Hi, Dick Thompson," or, "Nice to meet you, Dick." This helps you put a face with a name. Next time you run into Dick or speak with him on the phone, you will remember his name.

An interview usually begins with small talk. This is where an employer is getting to know you and giving you a chance to get settled. Participate in this talk. This gives you a chance to prove your people skills and wit. If you have a story to share, feel free to do so as long as it is appropriate for the setting. This gets the interviewers on your side. Keep the subject matter light. Let the employer guide the conversation. Be aware of the body language within the room. This will tell you when the interviewer is ready to start.

Preparation

Nothing looks worse to the employer than being unprepared. If you are not prepared for the interview, then your future could be uncertain. All companies have a history, and it is beneficial to know a little about it. Do your research. Most companies have a Web site, so familiarize yourself with the company before going into your initial interview. Try to acquaint yourself with the organization's mission statement. Also make note of key names and dates. Examples may be founders of the company or grand opening dates. Show your interest in the company history. After all, you are there to look into joining the "family."

Take extra copies of everything that you have given the employer before, such as your references and résumé. Even if the employer does not ask for one, it is good to have a copy with you. They can be used as a reference if need be. The interviewer may have been in a rush and forgotten or misplaced his or her copy, but if you arrive prepared, you will have a copy ready to hand him or her. This shows a sense of organization on your part.

Diana Podmoroff has written a book, 501+ Great Interview Questions for Employers and the Best Answers for Prospective Employees. Throughout Podmoroff's book, she describes the interviewing process from the interviewer's perspective. This viewpoint is important to the interviewee for a variety of reasons. Her book gives great insight into what the interviewer is looking for, and that gives you a distinct advantage. If you know where the interviewer is coming from and what he or she wants from you, then you are able to give the interviewer exactly that. Excerpts from Podmoroff's book are used throughout the remaining chapters of this book, so you can look at the interviewing process from different perspectives.

Podmoroff said, "From the moment the candidate walks in the door to the moment he or she leaves, the interview needs to follow a set, but somewhat flexible, script. From the introductions to the question-and-answer period to the final good-bye, the interviewer must remain in control, and the best way to ensure that is through planning and preparedness. This is not to imply you should deliver interview questions like a robot, or read from your piece of paper with hardly a glance at the person; the intention is to make the interview a smooth and objective process, facilitating a natural conversation within predetermined boundaries. This way the interviewer gains the information he or she needs, and the interviewee's responses can be compared to other candidates' responses quite easily."

Podmoroff is unfolding the fact that everyone needs to be on his or her toes during the interview process. Joseph McCormack answers, "Yes," to the question, "Can you tell if someone is prepared for an interview?" He goes on to say, "It's apparent from their knowledge of the hiring organization and/or the position and its responsibilities." Craig Fowler answers the question by saying, "Absolutely! It shows in the questions that they ask me. If they are prepared, they have relevant questions to ask me. They have an understanding of our niche and how we approach the physician-recruiting marketplace."

Here are two different men from two completely different organizations stating that it is imperative to come completely prepared for your interview. Do not get caught with you pants down in regards to these issues. Come with the knowledge and ability to conquer any questions that might be asked of you. If you do the proper research, it shows during the process. Go over your résumé, and be sure to address any time lapses that may be evident. Keep yourself out of the way of an embarrassing moment that may come with questions being asked that you are unprepared for.

You need to be equipped to take over the floor when it is your turn. Come to the interview with pre-thought out questions. Do research and find out what concerns you about the company. In addition, what information is lacking that you would like to know more about. If you are ill-equipped this does not speak well of your attentiveness. Coming to an interview unprepared also eliminates one of the few chances to find out what you specifically want to know about your position and the company. Most organizations provide you with a job description. No matter how lengthy or vague the descriptions are, you usually come away with questions. These questions are perfect questions to ask during the interview.

Coming prepared for an interview shows your ability to organize. Obviously, you are not going to be able to bring a whiteboard to your interview. However, you may have a calendar with you or your planner. Let the interviewer know, through example, that you are an organized individual. During the interview, you may ask if it is all right to take notes. It is always polite to ask before you start jotting things down. Most employers see this as a sign of organizational techniques. Writing down notes not only shows the employer your preparedness, but also helps you in the decision-making process. It is always a great idea to bring plenty of writing utensils. This way you are prepared with extras in case you drop one, or the interviewer has forgotten one. This keeps you in the interviewer's minds as prepared and caring.

Make sure to have enough questions and more to fill the time the company has allotted for your personal inquiries. As the saying goes, "No question is a stupid question." This saying usually rings true but try to be selective. No one wants to hire someone who is too self-involved and/or only cares about days off and vacations. This is where common sense comes into play.

Composure

Make sure to meet the interviewer's eyes when answering questions. Keep you hands in your lap. Do not fidget. Everyone is aware that this is a nerve-wracking process. However, it is important to try to stay comfortable and composed. You want to remain calm, and answer the questions accordingly. It is OK if you do not know the answer to a particular question. You are human, and the interviewers realize this. If you are feeling overwhelmed and do not know the answer to a question, ask the interviewer to repeat it. When the interviewer is finished repeating the question answer accordingly, or if you still do not have an answer, say exactly that. Maybe the interviewer will ask another similar question or just move forward. The person you know best is yourself so be confident. An interview is all about you. You are the master of knowledge about yourself.

Keeping composed is difficult. Before an interview if your nerves are getting to you, take control of the issue. Depending on your situation, exercise can be beneficial exercise. Sometimes it can take away some of the anxiety one might feel. Another topic to focus on is your breathing before the process begins. In many cases before an interview, you spend some time in a waiting area. Be prepared for this, and take something with you to distract you from the pressure you may feel. Looking over the job description or nervously trying to memorize your résumé is not going to help with your anxiousness. Bring a magazine, crossword puzzle, or something inconspicuous. This keeps your mind focused on something other than what lies in store.

Westly Kuser speaks about composure when asked, "During an interview what are the key qualifications you are looking for?" He comments: "Prior experience and willingness to learn are the most important qualifications in my line of work. I also look for employees that are open-minded and work well in teams. I need someone on my staff that has a good business sense." This shows that your ability to be flexible and want to take on new tasks motivates employers. Show them that the position in which you are interviewing for excites you and you are willing to take on any tasks that they bring your way.

Take these comments as pointers into your interview process. Show a sense of natural confidence. Do not completely let your guard down, but keep the employer aware that you are sure of yourself. No one is more confident in your abilities than you are. Do not let the employer down by straying away from your own self-assurance.

Joseph McCormack describes nerves in the following way when asked,

"Does the pace of the interview change if the candidate is noticeably nervous?" He answers, "I do my very best to put a candidate at ease because I believe that a relaxed candidate will be more forthcoming and honest than one under stress. If I sense that a candidate is nervous, I tell personal stories or leaven the conversation with humor. It helps to break up the "hard" interview questions with a bit of conversation from time to time."

So try to calm your nerves and keep composed. Chances are the interviewer himself is a bit nervous. Everyone tends to be panicky when he or she meets new people. Approach the interview as a conversation, and try to get to know the person as you might at a cocktail party. Avoid all the usuals: politics, religion, sex, and race. You are trying to show yourself off in your best light. Think of this as a dressing room, and do not bare all flaws.

Podmoroff writes, "By the time a potential employee gets to the interview stage, he or she better have all the technical skills and abilities necessary, otherwise you are wasting your time. The interview is the place to analyze the so-called 'soft' skills that are not easily amenable to testing. The absence or presence of these skills is what leads to the diagnosis of such common job maladies as poor interpersonal skills, an attitude problem, and personality conflict, unable to work in a team, poor communication skills, and problem with authority. Some individuals truly are difficult and hard to get along with, but most, if given the right environment, are very able to adapt and fit into a workplace that is right for them."

Podmoroff is describing the need to be prepared for an interview. You have jumped through the necessary hoops to get you here, and now you need to perform accordingly. As important as it is to be skilled, you also need to have people skills. Use the mannerisms you were taught as a child. Be polite. Ask yourself, "Is this the correct answer to the question?" before you blurt out your answer. Do not be afraid to use your charming smile either. As long as you are not cheesy, everyone will be pleased if they feel you are content and comfortable.

Chances are the group will be smaller, so use your interpersonal skills accordingly. Conduct the conversation on a more personal level. Do not approach the interview as if it were a speech. No one wants to be "preached" to. The "soft" skills that Podmoroff refers to are your one-on-one skills and your ability to conduct yourself within a group. Give examples of work situations when you preformed extraordinarily with a group. Did your last job consist of a group environment? Let this be known. Do you hold leadership skills? Do these characteristics come out during group work? If you have examples of this type of behavior, share this with the hiring manager. In the corporate environment, everyone enjoys a team player.

Show the employer your ability to fit in well with others. This can be shown by your communications skills, and how you hold yourself and your style of dress. If the work environment you are interviewing in is full of business suits, wear a business suit. This shows your ability to conform to the company's standards. This is not to necessarily say, "If everyone else is doing it, then you should too." Instead, it is pointing out that you do not want to look and act as if you are an outsider. Make sure to show your individuality while keeping the team's goals at heart. Prove to the employer that you are an enjoyable person with a positive outlook.

2

Work Environment

The environment in which you work is essential to your happiness at work. There are many different types of work environments, and not all environments suit all people. Knows where and how you work best. For instance, I work better in a quiet environment. Sometimes I enjoy light music, as not to have dead silence, but I cannot work well in a chaotic or crowded room with lots of conversations going on all around me. Also, I work better and faster in the mornings. I get most of the heavy work done between the hours of 7 a.m. and 2 p.m.. It is important for me that I work where all of these requirements are met. Otherwise, I will not be of much use to the company. Look out for yourself and the employer by researching the job's atmosphere and conditions before you arrive.

During an interview, you need to make yourself aware of your surroundings. Do you feel comfortable within this environment? Make a mental note of what you are feeling within the companies' atmosphere. Familiarize yourself with your surroundings. Ask questions such as:

What are your hours of operation?

This can be a tricky question. You do not want to come off as if you are only concerned about when you are able to leave, so make sure you ask this question at the correct time. It is important to find out the hours of operation for a variety of reasons. Depending on where you live in conjunction to where the office is located. You may have children that have to be at school at a particular time and you are their only ride. As mentioned earlier you may simply be a morning person. The list could go on and on but hours of operations are important. Make certain that you do not come off as if you are unwilling to work overtime.

How many people are employed within this company?

Numbers are imperative in the work environment. You know whether you work well in larger groups or smaller ones. Before you enter the interview, you have probably done your research here. However, you should not hesitate to ask the question. Web sites are not always accurate and things can change on a dime, so keep this question on the top of your list. The number of employees can help to make your ultimate decision. Different people work better in different work environments.

Whom will I be working with the majority of the time?

Here you are looking out for yourself. This question helps you find out important aspects of the position. Depending on the position you are interviewing for, you may or may not know who will be your "right-hand man." Knowing whom you will be working with on a day-to-day basis can give you great insight. Ask yourself whether or not you will enjoy the people they are listing. Personalities must mesh well to make your workday enjoyable.

What type of office environment will I be in?

If a cubicle is unacceptable in your mind, then asking this question is essential. You need to know what your surroundings are going to be. All offices operate differently, and your comfort is going to affect your work. So go into the interview prepared to let your views and expectations be known. However, do not overstep your boundaries. The people in the interview may be in the exact environment that you consider to be unpleasant.

You may want to find out more about certain aspects of your everyday work habitat. It might worry you that you are did not see pay periods on the job description. How is the work environment set up? Will you be at your desk all day, or will there be room to move around? What are the other employees like? Do you have regularly scheduled weekly meetings? Are there deadlines that are set in stone for your work? The answers to these questions will help you in the decision-making process. You want to make sure you are well-informed before taking on a position that you cannot handle or you do not want to handle.

Here you find out where you will work within the office. Workplaces differ in style. You want to be aware of whether you will have your own office with a door, or if you will be surrounded by others in a cubicle. If the workplace provides private offices, and you prefer to be around others, this is something to look into. If you are going to be working in a cubicle, find out who will be your neighbor. Are the cubicle walls high, or are they low? You should find out all of these things during the initial interview. You do not want to be shocked later on down the line.

Learning about your employee rights is essential to the interviewing process. You want to make sure that the company you are applying with is devoted to diversity.

Equal Opportunity Employment

Regardless of whether you are considered a minority, an equal-opportunity employer (EOE) is something that you should be looking for. EOEs give everyone a fair chance at advancement. Despite where you are from, whether you are male or female, EOEs must give you equal chances as anyone else within the company. This means that the employer has no right to discriminate. If you do not see in any of the documentation that the organization you are interviewing with is an EOE, make sure to ask the question.

Is your organization an Equal Opportunity Workplace?

The answer to this question helps you gain insight into what the company is like. Knowing that you will have a fair chance at voicing your own opinion within the workplace is relaxing. You probably do not want to join an organization where you are unsure about whether or not your opinions and ideas matter. If something comes up in the future that you disagree with, you might want to make sure that your opinion will be heard.

Employers value diversity, and this plays into teamwork. When working in teams, you are often among diverse groups of people. Are you open to diversity? Express your values in terms of how they affect your beliefs in diversity. Finally, if the organization is not an EOE you may want to consider other options.

Teamwork

Teamwork is something that is proven effective in the workplace. I was lucky to have teamwork instilled from an early age. I grew up in public school and played sports. All of my life, teamwork was always something my superiors stressed. Podmoroff said it best when she said, "Working in a team environment is almost a mainstay of modern work. Whether the team is formally recognized, long-term, short-term, or simply a group of people working toward a common goal, the ability to work with others is imperative. Working within a team context is unique in that all members are equally valued; a team environment is the sharing of resources and expertise that makes for enhanced production. It is also a prime situation for differences in opinions, styles of work and other interpersonal issues to surface. What you are looking for is a person who recognizes the value of teamwork and understands that to be effective, all members must collaborate. The result of this collaboration is called "synergy," because the team's output is better than the performance of the individual team member. Questions in the teamwork section focus on what the candidate believes to be true about effective teams, and what role he or she has played on effective and ineffective teams."

Teamwork is essential in most work environments. Let the employer know that you value teamwork and show them examples of when you have been in a team environment and have accomplished something satisfactory. Are you usually the chosen leader in a team? Why is that? Let the interviewer know about experiences when you were successful as a team member. Show that you are comfortable with the idea of synergy and tell them that teamwork excites you. Do you feel that when everyone works together great things happen? Be sure to let this be clear at the interview. Everyone loves a team player. Do not get stuck in a trap when the employer asks you if you prefer working alone or individually.

Tactically explain to the employer that you benefit from time with the team. Most companies require some form of teamwork. Even if you feel that your position is better suited for individual work, when you are a part of something bigger than just you teamwork is pertinent. Let the employer know that you understand the value of more than one brain working together. Describe to him or her circumstances in which you have seen the power of a team firsthand. Give him or her a chance to see that you want to work in this team environment and are happy to work toward a mutual goal.

Examples of prior teamwork always go over well. Regardless of your experience, chances are you have previously been on a team. Whether it is a sporting team, an academic team, a church group team, most people have been involved in teamwork throughout their lives. I went to a private university my first two years of college. The university's main focus was business. Therefore, we found ourselves forming teams on a regular basis. Sometimes our professors let us choose our teams. Other times, they randomly chose our teammates for us.

This was disconcerting at times, considering there are always some people you would rather not have on your team for one reason or another. For one particular project, I was paired up with three other individuals. These individuals seemed to be disinterested in the assignment. Upon our first meeting, nothing was negotiated. No tasks were assigned. Therefore, when it came time to our second meeting no real work had been done. I decided to take the situation into my own hands.

I consider myself to be somewhat of a passive person when it comes to groups, but I saw a real problem arising, and my grade was in jeopardy. Finally, I delegated tasks and deadlines. I gave team members their assignments, and let them know it had to be completed in full by our next meeting. Everyone was hesitant at first, but to my surprise, they took my direction. When our next meeting came around everyone was excited to meet up and share what he or she had accomplished. Our presentation ended up being a success, and we all did well that semester.

This shows that sometimes you have to read a situation, and take it into your own hands. Usually people do well when they are told what to do. Confusion comes along when there are no assigned tasks. So let the employer know that you are not afraid to tackle an assignment. Show them you care by giving an example of a time when you took a project by the reins, and delegated tasks and finished successfully.

Podmoroff's next point was, "One of the main challenges of working within a team is getting and maintaining cooperation. The whole idea of teamwork is to bring together different opinions and perspectives in the hopes of creating a better outcome than any one person could come up with. These interpersonal differences are what make coming to a consensus so difficult. What you are evaluating is the candidate's appreciation of these differences and what strategies he or she uses to handle the mixture constructively. Of particular interest is the role the individual plays in the situation. Do they tend toward mediator, reconciliatory, judge, compiler, evaluator, etc.? Evaluate the answer in terms of fit with the current team as well as appropriateness of the role."

Which role do you fit into? Podmoroff discusses the personality types that consist within teams. Before the interview, evaluate yourself. Find out which role your personality fits. Do you find yourself in the mediator position? Are you always trying to get the team to come together, and use all the ideas mentioned? Alternatively, are you more the reconciliatory type? Does your usual role in a group consist of keeping the team on the same page, and maintaining the arguments and keeping misunderstandings to a minimum? Do you usually take on the role of judge? Are the ideas of everyone in the team partial to your opinion? Do you find you are self-agreeing with all the others in the team regardless of their ideas? On the other hand, finally, is your role to evaluate all sources before coming to a conclusion?

Regardless of your race, color, or religion, equal-opportunity employment is a key factor. Finding a workplace that is accepting of all people is pertinent in the employment process. After all good teams are made up of all different sorts of individuals. Without variety, there would be no teams. Everything would be robotic and no new ideas would be brought to the table.

Diversity

Diversity is the force of America. Two heads are better than one and five heads are better than two are. In order for today's companies to be successful, they need input from all sources. This means that, if a company is made up strictly of white males, then it is not seeing all sides. This is not be considered a diverse organization. Not all sides are represented in this case. An all-male company's opinions are biased based on their employee make up, and that is not what America stands for.

During your interview, be careful to look at the faces that surround you. Does everyone look alike? Is your face the only different one in the room? Is there clearly a diverse group in front of you? This is something you should take into consideration. Your progress may or may not be decided upon this, but it is not something to take lightly. Be aware of you surroundings. Do not let the interview pressures harbor you blind.

The following is a list of a few questions that you should ask the employer pertaining to EOE.

Can I be sure the company is devoted to diversity and equal opportunity?

No matter what your sex, race, or religion, this is essential question. Here, you are making sure that everyone in this particular workplace is treated equally, and there is no separation concerning race, sex, or religious beliefs. Employers should be open and honest when answering this question. Make sure they elaborate on the subject so you can decipher whether or not they are telling the truth.

How do you describe the philosophy of the company or organization?

This question can help you get an idea of the company's viewpoint. It is important to find out the backbone of the organization, and decide if you agree with it and want to stand for that philosophy. If the employer tells you that he or she believes in the company's philosophy, and describes it in a fashion to which you do not agree, maybe this is not the place that best fits you. This is a decision you are going to have to live with for a while. If you do not agree with the company's values and beliefs, then you are not the right fit. You do not want to be working for an organization in which you feel like the odd man out.

Can you describe the work environment here?

Having someone else describe the work environment for you gives you some insight into whether or not the environment is noisy, fun, relaxed, hectic, quite, peaceful – you name it. Depending on where and with whom you like to work, the answer to this question lets you in on what type of setting you may be coming into. It can therefore help you to decide to take the position or not. If you are the type of person who needs to be in an enclosed space to accomplish anything, and you find that at this company you will be spending your time in a cubicle with all sorts of people around you, you may want to look elsewhere for employment. Otherwise, if you enjoy the camaraderie of an office and need other people to bounce your ideas off, this question is helpful in learning if this organization is going to create that type of atmosphere for you.

What attracted you to this organization?

Here is another icebreaker. A friendly question helps you see some of the positive, playful aspects of the organization. The answers could range from location, the line of work, the benefits, or the people. Any and all of these answers can help you make your ultimate decision.

You want to make sure that people are included in the answer to the question. It is extremely important to be surrounded with others who are fun, loving, and ambitious. Diversity is also a key factor. As mentioned earlier, a diverse organization is where you want to be.

Assignments & Tasks

When looking into working for an organization, it is imperative to realize what types of assignments and tasks you will be given. After all, assignments and tasks make up your workday. Having a clear understanding of what your responsibilities are going to be makes your decision-making process much easier. When the employer explains the responsibilities that will be thrown your way, you can assess the situation accordingly. The employer may not be able to list each task that will be performed on a daily basis, but he can at least give you an idea of what lies ahead.

Do these assignments and tasks appeal to your sensibilities?

Here you want to asses whether or not you feel that the assignments and task appeal to you. If all aspects sound attractive then you are golden. However, if some portion sounds dreadful, you need to consider this. Knowing whether you can handle the task is one thing. Nevertheless, make sure the assignments sound appealing. After all, you will be tackling these tasks on a daily basis.

Exactly, what am I going to be doing on a daily basis?

It seems that, throughout my interviewing experience, I have never been able to find out just what exactly I would be doing. From brief job descriptions that one might find on a search engine to unsure answers from upper management, this is not something you should take lightly. It is hard to be pushy during an interview, but sometimes it is necessary. If you are asking questions and not getting complete answers, do not hesitate to ask questions that are more precise. This is what the interview process is about. Again, this is not only the interviewer's time to question you. You are there for the same reasons they are. The process is all about finding out if you are a fit for their company and if they are the right fit for you.

Job descriptions are often vague. When an employer does not describe all the details of a position, it is impossible to know whether or not you will enjoy all aspects of your daily work. Do not go away empty handed on this question. Find out when, where, how, with whom, and why you are going to do the tasks you are given. This helps everyone in the process to determine whether this position is right for you. If all but one aspect of the position sounds wonderful, but that one thing will keep you up at night, then the position is not right for you. On the other hand, if you feel that you can handle and, more importantly, enjoy doing all facets of the job, then jump on board.

During the normal workday, employees receive a variety of assignments. Not all the details of a position are disclosed during the interview process. Your decision is going to be influenced according to the assignments and task. Regardless of whether these assignments include creating graphs, doing research, or stocking shelves, the list could be continuous. It is hard to describe every detail of the workday. This is not because the employer is trying to hide certain aspects of the position; rather, it is often impossible to divulge all aspects of the workday. That said, try to pinpoint things that might discourage you during the workday. You may want to ask questions pertaining to potential dilemmas to help you in the decision-making process.

Competency and Fit

Podmoroff describes competency and fit in the following terms: "Companies are notorious for hiring based on skill and ability, and firing based on fit. Many interviewers make the mistake of equating knowledge, skills, and ability (KSA) with competency. Competency is more closely related to an individual's suitability to the workplace than their actual education and experience. If you are hiring for a graphic artist, candidates can be easily eliminated based on their education, experience, and portfolio of work. These factors are prerequisites for developing competency, but none of them (alone or in combination) can ensure that the candidate will indeed perform the job at the level you deem suitable. The final component in determining competency is the fit factor, and the best way to evaluate a candidate's overall competency is to screen for skill and ability and interview for competency and fit."

Podmoroff is describing how the employer has done the initial screening practice. He or she has done so by going over the original screening procedure. Maybe you have turned in your résumé with a list of references. These items show that you are suitable for the position, but now you need to show the employer with your words and actions that you are actually fit for the position. After the interviewer sees that you have the skills and the abilities to conquer the position, they now want you to show them that you fit in with their team. Every work environment is different. Therefore, you need to do enough research on the company so that you are aware how to actually fit into the role that you desire to fill.

If you are experienced in one field or another and your résumé does not elaborate on that particular skill, make sure to touch on this fact during the interview. The employer already knows what is on your résumé. This interview is your time to shine. Tell him or her what is not already on that piece of paper. Let him or her know by your actions that you desire this position, and you have the skills to be successful. Show him or her that you are a team player, and you are eager to join the group.

What type of position are you interviewing for? Do you feel comfortable with all aspects of the position? Are you uncertain about what you will be doing during most of the day? Is this a sales position? Will you be cold calling people? These are all questions you want to ask yourself and the interviewer. The answers to these questions and more can help you down the road. It is important to be self-aware before you begin the interviewing process. Otherwise, you are likely to be swayed one way or the other. This is because, if you do not go into the process with your mind made up, there is nothing firm about your stance.

Podoromoff describes, "The entire list of competencies for any job will, of course, be different according to the job itself and the level of responsibility. A plumber must have expert plumbing skills whereas a computer programmer does not, but they both need to be able to communicate well and handle stress appropriately. The key competencies presented in this book are a compilation of the most common skills required to be successful on the job."

She goes on to state, "Not every job will need all the competencies but most jobs will require most competencies."

To eliminate waffling try to ask yourself what you feel the answers should be to the following questions. If the employer's answers match up with your own, then you may have found a job worth keeping.

Upon being hired, what types of assignments will I be given?

Here is where you are able to see directly into the tasks that the company is going to hand you. If the answer is something you think sounds interesting, this might just be a match. Asking this question helps you gain insight into the day-to-day activities that are in your near future if you are hired. Everyone wants to be sure of what situations he or she is walking into.

Is it possible for me to obtain a written description of the position?

Asking for a written description of the job not only shows the employer that you are interested in every aspect of the position; it also helps you in your decision-making process. Many times, something is overlooked. A written description is always a good tool to have. You can go over it at home when you need a refresher.

Can you tell me more about my day-to-day responsibilities?

This is the kicker. It is extremely important to find out exactly what your employer expects of you on a day-to-day basis. This is where you are going to be spending a large part of your life. It is imperative to know what those hours are going to consist of. Many times, the person giving you the interview may not know all the details of the job. In a case where you are going to fill an administrative position and you are speaking with the top executive, you may want to ask for more feedback. If the person giving you the interview is unable to give you a complete answer, it is not wrong to ask for some research to be done and for them to get back with you. You want to be sure that this is a role you are willing to fill. If part of your day consists of filling the coffee pot for the other executives, it is imperative that you evaluate the situation and ask yourself if this is something, you are willing to do. If you think that, in a couple of months, dealing with other people's morning beverages is going to bother you, make sure to consider those.

What happens when an assignment is finished?

Here, you find out the process in which you go about turning things in, as well as where to go to get your next assignment. This helps you familiarize yourself with the organization's flow and gain insight into who you will be working with.

Can you please explain the company's organizational structure?

With this question, you are asking the employer to explain the chain of demand. Who works under whom and so forth? Knowing who the main chief of staff is may help in your decision-making process. This all depends on your opinion of the individuals.

What types of tasks do you feel will be the most important for me to accomplish on a day-to-day basis?

Here you find out your number one responsibilities. Do you find these tasks to be interesting and important? If so then you should have no worries. However, if you find the listed task to be dull and daunting, this is a warning sign.

I am an extremely motivated person. I do not take well to not completing a task. Do you feel that I have the height of persistence needed to fit into this organization?

This question is "tooting your own horn" a bit. But, sometimes it is necessary in the "interrogation room." Prepare yourself with a stack full of questions that may lead to your benefit in a tense moment.

Podmoroff describes an efficient employee as an "organized one." She says, "The ability to establish a course of action for yourself (and/or others) is essential for accomplishing goals thoroughly and on time. Organization requires proper planning of assignments and allocating resources. Time spent organizing and planning will ensure steps are not missed, timelines are met, and tasks are prioritized. To be well-organized, a person must employ particular tools and techniques. Look for evidence that the candidate uses a variety of strategies to remain focused."

Podmoroff goes on to give examples, including:

- Daytimer
- Planning calendars

- To-do lists
- Flow charts
- Timelines
- Scheduling software
- Whiteboards
- Filing systems
- Regular meetings
- Visual planning software (e.g., GAANT charts)

What is the Company's Mission Statement?

A company's mission statement shows you what the organization truly stands for. You want to make sure you have all the same beliefs. If you disagree with a company's mission statement, you and the company will not be working toward a common goal. Therefore, it is not going to work out between you and the employer. You have to find a position in which you agree and believe in the mission statement.

How does the current management style compare to other places of work?

This question leads you to finding out if this particular company's managers tend to micromanage or if they give their employees more freedom. Knowing whether your manager is going to continuously look over your shoulder should help you in determining if this is the correct position for you. It is usually satisfying to get away from the norm. You may be excited if the employer goes over a different way of doing things than you are used to. Be cautious and make sure all the ideas that are mentioned make sense.

What are your suggestions for someone who is trying to find a career in your line of work?

Ken Sundheim answers, "Similar to any field, you must be cautious of the type of employment agency you choose. Some recruiting firms are great and are full of intelligent, successful people. However, because there is a low entry bar and minimal base salary, many firms are not selective about their employee pool and are unpleasant places to work. They often see their success and financial resources quickly drained.

When entering the field, it is best to begin with a specialty and get very good at it. You have to think to yourself, "Do I want to be in law recruitment, sales recruitment, technology recruitment or some other facet?" You should go with what interests you. If you do not like computers, stay away from IT recruiting firms.

I would also suggest reading a book on recruiting. Being a headhunter is not for everyone. In most cases, there is no steady paycheck, as most firms provide health insurance and pay on commission; you must prepare yourself for that. Be aware that this business is very competitive and economically sensitive. When the times are good, they are great and when corporate hiring slows, it seems as if the office is a ghost town. Get to know the lay of the land as well as the ups and downs before diving into recruitment."

Ken is telling us that we should make sure we feel that the career is a fit before we move forward in the process. This is another example of how research can come into play and benefit us in the end. Ken gives you questions to ask yourself about the field you are going to be interviewing in. It cannot hurt to take his suggestions, go to the local library, and check out a book. If there is one thing, I have learned it is not to walk into an interview "empty headed." Employers find it obvious if you do not know about their field.

Throughout my interview experience, I have realized that until you actually get to the interview you do not know what you are facing exactly. However, even still being prepared with knowledge about the industry is imperative. Give yourself a leg up on your competition and do your homework. There is nothing more embarrassing then being asked a simple question about the line of work in which you are interviewing and not being able to come up with a single answer. Show your dedication to your line of work by researching the company and its industry surroundings.

Deadlines

Finally, we are forced to focus on deadlines. Podmoroff says, "Deadlines are inevitable and can be stress inducing if you do not plan adequately for full completion of a project. What you want to know is how well the candidate responds to deadlines and what factors contributed to missed deadlines. Of equal importance is the recognition that quality and completion should not be rushed just to make a deadline. Communication is important in all projects, and you should look for evidence that the candidate keeps all stakeholders informed about the progress and status of a project. This type of process will more often result in modified deadlines rather than missed ones."

Deadlines are expected. What Podmoroff is saying here is that the employer wants to make sure you see the importance of deadlines and are always well-prepared. Everyone knows that things come up during the day that keep you from certain projects. Therefore, it is important to plan for these types of disturbances. Unless there is an emergency, it is not acceptable to miss a deadline. Let the employer know that you understand this and believe in it. No one wants an incomplete assignment. They also do not want one that has not been finished to its complete potential. Show the employer that you are aware of both of these aspects and that you do not foresee yourself getting behind on deadlines. Let them know that you are the type of person that does not let obstacles get in your way of meeting deadlines. This should lead the employers to feeling at ease if you become their choice for hire.

Rules and Regulations

Here are a few words from Podmoroff about organizational rules: "All workplaces operate within a set of rules. Some workplaces are more structured than others are, but there is always a fundamental set of rules and regulations that apply. Some rules are explicit and others may be cultural, or 'that's the way it's done around here.' The compliance section allows you to determine a candidate's respect for and adherence to these rules."

Ask the employer about the company's rules and regulations:

What types of rules do you have that I may need to be aware of?

Show the employer that you respect their rules and regulations. Do not hem and haw over the organization's procedures. All organizations have certain guidelines that they follow. Finding out what certain rules apply keeps you well-informed about what types of regulations have to be followed at this company. Rules and regulations are what make a place work. Getting to know what guidelines that have to be followed lets you recognize whether or not you are willing and able to do so. This may ultimately lead to a decision.

Let the employer know that you only feel satisfied with your day's work if you have completed all the tasks that have been set in front of you. Do not give them any room to think that you may only be there for the paycheck. Of course, most everyone goes to work with the goal of being paid. Yet, you can show them that you have chosen to interview with their company because you feel a sense of satisfaction after completing the assignments given to you. Let them know why you are interested in the particular position and what you feel you will gain from it. This will show the employer that you are not just in it for the green.

Chain of Command

Organizational Structure

When working for a corporation, there is always a chain of command. The chain of command represents the levels of the organization. It is important to know where you stand. What is your place on this organization's totem pole? Many organizations want you to believe everyone is on an equal playing field. This is a pleasant approach, but it does not give you the answer you are looking for. When looking for employment, you set yourself up for success. Is the position you are applying for at the top of the ladder? Do you fit in the middle? Or are you at the very bottom?

There is nothing wrong with being at the bottom of the ladder. It is just something that you need to be keenly aware of. No matter where you fall in the organizational structure, you want to find out who your immediate supervisor will be. Knowing who you are going to report to may help you in the decision making process. It seems that, when working for someone that you admire and respect, the workday is easier. This way you are comfortable taking constructive criticism from this individual. On the other hand, if you are going to be working under someone with whom you feel incompetent, getting along is going to be very difficult.

Getting to know an organization's structure helps in seeing how and why the company works the way, it does. Furthermore, when we know whom we will be working with and whom we will be working directly under, we feel more comfortable with the situation. Strive to be well-informed about whom you will be working under and where you will be in the marching order.

Will I have to consistently report to upper management or am I going to be able to initiate work on my own?

Where and to whom you are going to have to report are great answers to have. This question relates to how the company operates. Micromanagement is something that few people enjoy. Some find it necessary but you need to ask yourself if you can work in a micromanagement position.

Probing

Podmoroff writes, "The conversation will inevitably shift to the person's comfort zone and to the area of development in which he or she feels most confident. Make a note of the impression the candidate wants to give from the start, and then make sure to probe fully into questions that deal with the areas not emphasized. The more well-rounded a person, the higher the chances of being able to deal with the changes and interpersonal skills required in most work environments."

So be prepared for personal questions. Perhaps you are in the process of moving and want to sound more stable. Prepare answers for these types of situations. If you are looking into this job because you have recently been divorced and you are relocating, you do not have to share this type of information. Instead, bring your more positive elements to the table. That is not to say be ashamed of what is going on in your life. However, just as you may not want to know about a date's baggage at first glance, an employer wants to hear about more positive aspects of your personal life. Give them examples of your love for your children and dedication to your family.

"Interpersonal skills are the broad range of skills that allow people to communicate effectively, build rapport, and relate well to all kinds of people. Listen for self-awareness, understanding, and an ability to communicate effectively with others regardless of differences. Be sure to probe for as many details and specifics as possible, such as names, dates, and other verifiable information. Skilled interviewers will also ask candidates for their thoughts or feelings about a situation to gain further insight."

Bill Puckett, of Searchline Services, Inc describes his favorite interview question: "I always like to ask the Candidate to tell me about a time in his or her life when they thought they were going to be killed.

The purpose of this question is that Candidates do a lot of acting and trying to be someone they think you are looking for and not be themselves. When they start telling a story about how they almost lost their lives, they get so emotionally involved in the story that they forget to act the part they are acting and they become more themselves. I have seen Candidates have completely different accents when they are telling me their life threatening story."

So be careful when approached with a question such as this one. Remember to keep yourself poised. You are under pressure, but you need to keep your composure when answering such a question as this. Here is what the interviewer is looking to gain from the conversation. If the interviewer then goes on to probe you for more information, this is when you give it. Do not voluntarily over share unless you feel that the situation awards this. When asking probing questions, interviewers have to be careful. Here is what four of our case studies answered when asked the question:

Do you ask about someone's personal life during an interview?

Ken Sundeheim of KAS Placement: "Within the bounds of legality, yes. I am interested in what motivated a candidate to choose his or her career, who has been a role model or influence, what they value in an employer, etc., Issues about health are only permissible within the context of ability to do a job, but questions about how a candidate handles stress, what he or she does to relax or recharge a depleted battery can lead to some interesting discussions. If travel is involved, we need to establish that this would not be a hardship for the candidate."

Craig Fowler of Pinnacle Health Group: "It usually comes up from their end. I train recruiters about EEOC (Equal Employment Opportunity Commission) questioning, so I do not make a habit of 'asking' about a candidate's personal life, as I want to avoid crossing any lines relative to marital status, age, religion, etc."

Michael R. Maffei of Brandon Wayne Group: "As an interviewer, I make it a point to stay away from personal questions unless they are common questions like where do you live, how was your Thanksgiving, etc. In human resources, you can get into a lot of trouble if you attempt to dig too deep into another's personal life."

Kristie Wehe of Weststaff: "Generally no, but it does depend on what position they are interviewing for, and the kinds of responses they give. Sometimes they lead you to ask questions. Usually if someone is moving into the area, I will ask him or her why."

To whom will you be reporting to throughout the workday? Is this person in the interview? Are you going to be your own boss? Where will you be bringing your ideas? The answers to these questions are pertinent. Finding out to whom and where you will be reporting is significant to your well-being. Do you respect your supervisor? Does he or she share the same admiration for you? Some of these answers are impossible to know off hand. However, you must ask yourself these questions. It is important to trust yourself and your gut feeling about the organization.

Who are the company's leaders, and how did they come upon that role?

The answer to this question shows you who is ranked where within the company. The employer should give you examples as to how the upper management obtained their positions. This helps you decide if you will be able to move up the ranks in an efficient manner.

Who would be my immediate supervisor?

Asking this question shows direct interest in whom you will be interacting with on a daily basis. It is important to know whom you are going to be reporting to. You will be looking to this person for direction and support.

Can you please give me a little insight as to whom I will be working with most closely?

Here is another direct question. The answer to this question gives you a good idea as to the personalities and departments you will be dealing with on a more frequent basis. This helps outline your daily schedule and informs you of different personalities throughout the workplace.

Where do finished assignments go?

The answer to this question goes along with organizational structure. In a large corporation, it is important to know the whereabouts of your work. When asking these types of questions you are showing your interest in the inner workings of the company.

Is there a certain area of your company where the most successful people come from? If so where?

Here is an interesting question. Most companies promote from within. It is always important to know if there is a leading position that is promoted. If so, you may want to make it clear that you would like to be promoted. Depending on whether that is, the position you have applied for or not it is always important to know.

How does the chain of command work within this particular corporation?

The answer to this question gives you insight on how this particular organization is run. It also gives you the ability to assess where you may wind up in the next few months or years. This shows you the overall process of the organization. With hard work, where do you see yourself in the future? If the employer explains that employees have to stay in a certain position for years to come without the possibility of advancement, you will have this to consider as well.

Feel free to use some or all of the questions, but make sure you use your own words. Of course, not all these questions have to be asked. These are just guidelines. Make sure to choose questions that can help you obtain the information that is specific to your needs and concerns.

Change

After answering the above questions there is something else, you need to consider change within the organization. Podmoroff has written, "Some organizations change rapidly and frequently, while others are less intense. For those companies where change is a permanent fixture, assessing a candidate's level of flexibility and adaptability is crucial."

Craig Fowler of Pinnacle Health Group answers the question, "What do you feel is the most important question in a job interview?" as, "'What is motivating you to make a change at this time?' This question will give the interviewer many directions to take the interview. It has the potential to give the interviewer a sense of the candidate's seriousness about making a change, it gives the interviewer insight as to how this person makes decisions, and it can give the interview a hint as to this person's attitude toward work."

If you are interviewing with an organization that changes on a frequent basis, it is important to show the employer that you are flexible and aware of change. Allow the interviewer to see how you adapt to a rapid environment. You may want to ask:

How frequently does the organization's daily routine change?

Here you find whether the organizational structure changes on a regular basis. Some people are more keen and acceptable to change. Others prefer a more mundane lifestyle. You know yourself and where you fit in best. Do not pick an organization that is rapidly changing if you are not someone who can operate in a chaotic environment. If you are young and up for any challenge then an organization that goes through progress and changes frequently might be more of your style.

What types of changes usually go on during the year?

Depending on what field you are going into, a question like this can keep you aware of when and where you will see change in your work life. Retail operations for example, have increased numbers, crowds, hours, and chaos during the holiday seasons. Other types of workplaces have their "busy season" as well. Very few organizations stay the same year round. So ask this question to better inform yourself of what is in store for the coming months.

Do you feel that I am capable of adapting with the changes?

Here you are putting your employer on the spot. Asking him this question may or may not throw him for a loop. Nevertheless, you want to make certain that the person you are interviewing with is interested in you and feels that you are capable of tackling the position at hand. Keep the question upbeat as not to sound like you are challenging your interviewer.

Podmoroff gives us a list of questions within this area of competency that are designed for the employer to assess the candidate's ability to deal with the following situations:

- Ambiguity

- Constraints

- Rapid change

- Frustration

- Shifting priorities

- Multiple demands

- Frustrating circumstances

- Identifying other's needs

- Putting other's needs first

Do you have the ability to handle rapid changes at the workplace? If not, this is OK. This particular employer may not be right for you. If so, let the employer know that these changes will not frustrate you. Show them that you are able to handle multiple demands at the same time. Give them examples of how you are able to identify the needs of others and handle them with ease. Let the employer know that you are capable of handling frustrating circumstances and constraints by giving him or her examples of when you have tackled multiple tasks under pressure.

Leadership

For instance, while I was in college I worked as a receptionist at a chain hotel. At midnight, if a guest does not show or call their room goes back into the "open" pool. One particular night all of the rooms were booked besides one. The one room was being held for a single guest. There must have been a large event in town because the hotel door seemed to be revolving.

Finally, the clock struck midnight and there was still no sign of the mysterious guest. I decided to give the room up to a family with young children. Not soon after the man showed up suitcase in hand, exhausted from delayed flight after delayed flight. Needless to say, there were no open rooms. Although I was flustered and there was chaos, I kept my cool. I explained the situation to the guest and to my surprise, he understood. After the explanation, I began calling our "sister" hotels in the area. I was persistent in trying to find him a room nearby. Luckily, a hotel down the road was able to accommodate the gentleman.

These situations happen often and it is how you handle the pressure that counts. The next day I explained the situations to my manager. I told her what happened and she appreciated my efforts. A few months down the road, I was in line for a promotion. Showing your calm under pressure can pay off in the end.

Podmoroff goes on to say, "Not all positions require formal leadership, but the characteristics of effective leaders are often desirable across a variety of positions. The important issue for you to uncover is the candidate's personal beliefs around what an effective leader does and how he or she goes about doing it. Whether the position is management or staff, you need to evaluate the candidate's ability to motivate and positively influence others in the workplace."

Here, Podmoroff is describing that the employer is interested in your personal beliefs on leadership. This is something you should prepare for before the interview. Do you enjoy being a leader? How do you normally go about leading others? Do you have a tremendous ability to influence others? If so, how do you go about doing so? Do people tend to look to you as a natural leader? How is this evident in your day-to-day life? Has someone told you in the past that you make an amazing leader? Do not hesitate to share these things and more during your interview. Keep the interviewer interested in your ability to lead others. Demonstrate your abilities throughout the interview.

If the interview does not seem to be going smoothly, try to change the direction of where the interview is heading. Show the employer that you have the ability and willingness to take control of the situation yourself. Here, you are showing the interviewer your leadership skills. Showing off your leadership attributes always helps during the interview process. Organizations normally enjoy someone who takes charge. Companies want someone who is not afraid to take the situation by the reins and lead the whole team to victory. It is important to be able to adapt to different situations and realize when something is not going your way. So, redirect the conversation and see if you can better display yourself in a different light.

If the Position Is Not Right For You

Assessment

During the interview process, you should assess every aspect of the situation. Ask yourself a variety of questions. Make note of your surroundings and your personal feelings throughout the interview. Be sure to take everything that is said into account. This will help you come decision-making time. If you are feeling wary of the situation, you may want to take a step back. Just because someone puts an offer on the table does not mean you have to take it.

Is this position something that has always interested you?

If you find yourself questioning every word coming out of the employer's mouth while they are interviewing you, this is a big red flag. During the interview process, you want to make sure that you agree with what the interviewer is saying. Just because you have made it in the door and last night, you were feeling positive about the position does not mean that this feeling has lasted through today. If your gut is telling you to flee the scene, this is something that you are going to have to consider.

It is disappointing when an interview does not go the way we expected it, and this is OK. It happens to everyone. There are always things we can look into better the next time. Do not take a position just because it is offered to you. If you were expecting flowers and coffee, you are being unrealistic. However, if you were expecting professionalism and you did not get it, this is no the right choice for you. During an interview, if you receive negative signs, you need to make note of them. Usually, we are so caught up in ourselves that we just brush over warning signs. Do not let this happen to you!

Make sure to go into an interview with a clear head. You need to take time to process all the information that is given to you over the course of the interview. When you go home that night, it might be a good idea to write down all the positive and negative aspects of the interview. This particular strategy is used in situations such as this because it works. The answer is usually staring you in the face. If the negative outweighs the positive, this is not the right position for you. There is no harm in deciding not to take a position that has been offered to you. You are not only helping yourself, but you are helping the employer in the end. The employer will not benefit from an employee who does not believe in their organization.

Challenges

Questions that you may consider asking the employer might be:

Can you foresee any challenges that you feel I am going to have to overcome if offered this position?

This is the employer's chance to tell you some of the more difficult aspects of the position. In addition, if the employer is having second thoughts, he or she can express them now. No one enjoys hearing negative things about themselves, but sometimes this is necessary. It not only makes you stronger, but it also lets you know where you stand.

You may have shared something personal during the interview process that offset the employer, and now he or she does not feel you are going to be the best fit. The only way to know this is to ask the question. You may then explain yourself more thoroughly. However, if you have shared something that the employer deems unacceptable, and it is something that you would never consider changing, than this is not the correct place for you.

For instance, you have children and are unable to travel. In addition, if you are unable to work the necessary overtime, then this is not a correct fit for you. It is better to find this out early on in the process rather than later. You will save yourself and the employer heartache as well as time.

Do you feel you are going to be able to defeat these challenges?

If so, there is nothing to worry about. If you are second-guessing yourself, try to think of strategies that might help you iron some of the situations out. If you still cannot seem to find a solution, maybe the position is not right for you.

Find out that you are not fit for a particular position is not easy on your ego. Nevertheless, do not let this get you down. Use each situation as an opportunity for you to learn. These experiences can never e a total loss. Take something with you that you can use in the future. This is after all about you.

How does your company handle direct criticism?

Most companies deal with criticism on a daily basis. This is evident in the competitive nature of society. It is crucial to know where the interviewing company stands on this issue. If you like to handle criticism head on, but the company you are interviewing with prefers to take a more lackadaisical approach, then you should consider this difference. Does the company's way of doing things conflict with your beliefs and practices? If so, this position may not be right for you.

Take for example, soft drink companies and political campaigns. These people usually go for the throat of their competitors. On more than one occasion, I have felt my jaw drop when watching these types of commercials. Is this the type of competitive nature that you possess? Find your answer and then ask yourself if this position is right for you.

Kristie Wehe of Westaff was asked, "How does your company compare to its competitors." She answered, "I think this is a great question, because if they can't tell you this right off the bat, something is wrong. And it's important to know if the interviewer at least believes that the company has a terrific reputation in the marketplace, if they are going to grow and continue to hire, etc. I chose Westaff because of their reputation, and the professionalism of the recruiter. And because, even though they weren't the biggest or the most well-known, they had a strong presence in the marketplace, and a solid reputation with both their candidates and their clients."

Are there any problems with the company that I should know about?

You are looking for the answer "no" here; but in case the answer is "yes," you should be aware the problems. If there are major problems that are going to put your job at risk in the near future, you need to be cautious. You are hoping for an honest answer here. If the employer gives you the run around or if they list problems that cannot be solved, this position is not right for you.

Look into the market before even walking through the door. If you are looking into a company that has recently laid off more than half of its employees then be wary. Downsizing is a vulnerable thing.

Are there certain qualities and characteristics that are necessary for someone to succeed in this job?

Here the employer may list attributes that he or she feels are obligatory in order to be successful in the position. If these qualities are close to yours, or if they are an exact fit, say so. If you do not possess any of the qualities, you might want to reconsider the position at hand.

For example, many entry level positions involve sales. Although the job description may not have implied sales, the position you are applying for may primarily be based on salesmanship. I have been to too many interviews which unexpectedly led to sales conversations. If this suites you, fine. However, if you are like me and not interested in selling, you may find this an important question.

How soon are you looking to fill this position?

Finding out when the employer is actually hiring gives you an idea of whether this position is a fit. If you are unemployed and are unable to pay your bills, this is something to consider. Sometimes companies interview for positions that will not be opening for months to come. If you have enough funds in the bank or you are currently employed, this may not be a deterrent for you. However, if you are not able to make ends meet without taking a job in the next few weeks, then you are left with a decision. After considering all these aspects, you may find that this position is not right for you.

Effective communication, regardless of the style, requires two important skills. All these questions can help you assess your ability and willingness to join an organization. They also show you more about an organization's structure. This gives you answers that might help you decide if an organization is right for you.

Is my position challenging?

Here is a plain and simple question that should get you a direct answer. Sometimes it is best to be straightforward with your interviewer. This way you are able to ask the questions you want and the employer can elaborate however, they please. Everyone wants to be challenged during the workday. Although sometimes we are stressed because of challenges, without them we would be completely bored.

I was once in a position where I did not feel challenged. I worked for a company creating car ads. Initially it took me awhile to learn the computer programs but once I mastered the task I found myself doing the same thing day in and day out. It got to the point where I dreaded going into work because each day was mundane. Work should be full of challenges. It should help you strive to be a better person. You should learn new skills and strive to move up the ladder.

Did the person that was previously in my position possess the skills to take on the position's day-to-day challenges?

Asking this question gives you more information about the position in which you are interviewing for. Why is the previous employee not there anymore? Has he or she been fired or promoted? Making yourself aware of the current situation you are looking into can only benefit you during your decision-making process.

Asking Questions

To fully understand a message being sent, and thus respond appropriately, a person must ask clarifying questions when necessary. Not asking questions eventually leads to misunderstandings, the root cause of most communication breakdowns.

Joseph McCormack gives us his insight to "the most important question for a candidate to ask." He explains, "After a candidate has exchanged pleasantries with the interviewer, I would ask, 'Before we begin, please tell me what the most important things are that you need to know about my background or experience for this position so that I can be focused and helpful in my responses to your questions.'"

Here is a problem that we can avoid during the interviewing process. There is no harm in asking questions. If you are unsure about a comment or a detail about the position, do not hesitate to ask. No question is a stupid question. You are at the interview for a reason. That reason is to get to know more about the position for which you are interviewing. In order to do so, you need to ask questions. You do not want to leave the interview with questions or misunderstandings. This interview serves a purpose for both you and the employer. You want to make sure your goals are obtained during the interview, as well as the employer's goals. So go ahead; ask the questions that you came prepared with.

The "perfect job" is it out there? I asked this question to Craig Fowler and here is his response, "No. Just like, there are no perfect candidates. Last time I checked, there are no perfect people alive today; and, by definition, a job has workers and supervisors who are imperfect people. Seriously, I tell candidates and clients, that if they have found 80 percent of what they are looking for in a job or a candidate, then they should strongly consider accepting the position or the candidate."

Another opinion is that of Peter M. Sorensen, President of Dane Contracting, Inc., Indialantic, Florida. Sorensen believes it is possible to find the perfect job. He states, "Yes, but it is rare in today's business place. Like in life, a good attitude toward your job can bring you happiness and wellbeing." Sorensen says this after being asked the question, "Is it possible to find the perfect job?"

Westley Kuer agrees with Sorensen, saying, "I think it is possible to find the perfect job, when you are paid to do something that you enjoy doing and are passionate about, it is not considered work."

It seems there are two different opinions here. As in most things, people do not always agree; but I think the final opinion of Michael Maffi sums it up best: "There is an old saying, Love what you do and then you will have the perfect job. Once you lose that feeling, then it just becomes another job."

This Company Is A Match!

During the interview, if you are having a great feeling about the company and your inner voice is saying, "Yes, this is great," this company may be a match for you. Listen to what your inner voice is telling you. If you enjoy those who are interviewing you and feel as if you are nailing all the questions, you may have found yourself a new employer. Be careful not to get overexcited. Just because you had, a great interview does not mean that the next person who walks through the door is not going to have a great interview as well.

Craig Fowler explains, "What makes you successful in your line of business?"

Persistence is probably the most important quality. Able to tolerate ambiguity is up there on the list of what makes recruiters successful. Another quality that is extremely important is remaining a student of the field/industry. Healthcare is an ever-evolving industry, constantly in flux. So, remaining up-to-date with information makes recruiters relevant and credible; these are qualities that are invaluable in our field.

Here Craig explains that your ability to stay up-to-date and interested in your line of work is imperative. When you lose interest, you lack motivation. If the motivation is not, there the work ethic, as well as the accountability, declines. Keep yourself interested by doing research and learning all that you can about your particular industry.

Motivation

What motivates you? This is a question you need to ask yourself. Are you motivated when you have deadlines that you have to meet? Do you enjoy the challenge of researching something until you find the correct answer? Are you able to motivate yourself by checking things off a list?

When you find the answers to these questions and more, then you are identifying factors that you like to see in your next position. If you feel that all aspects of this job are rewarding and they excite you, then you are probably motivated to begin performing the task. This will keep you in tune with the company. This company could be the one!

Here Podmoroff describes motivation: "An employee's motivation is one of the most important factors in employee productivity. A paycheck only motivates to a certain degree; after that, other factors need to be present to drive an employee to perform good work. Those other factors are the activities and responsibilities that provide personal satisfaction as well as job satisfaction. What you are looking for is an employee who is motivated to do a good job because he or she derives intrinsic satisfaction from knowing that a job was done well."

Bob Clark, CEO of Furst Group headquartered in Rockford, Illinois explains that his work "Most definitely" influences the lives of other people. "The work we do influences the lives of other people, because we are working to find the best candidates for jobs in the health care field. The executives we place manage major hospitals and health systems, managed care plans, medical groups, hospice organizations, specialty service, and insurance companies. They are at the forefront of medical care, and their decisions affect millions. So of course the work we do is taken with the utmost care and responsibility.

Our work also influences the lives of the candidate and their families as they often face relocation and a new career direction."

This statement and others like this one are motivators in themselves. It is great to hear that people feel that their time and efforts are beneficial to the lives of others. Motivating statements such as these give a person the drive to find the right career. Your work should reflect who you are as and individual. It is beneficial to everyone if you understand your role in society and feel as if it is a fit.

Qualifications

Podmoroff gives examples of "[s]igns that an employee is internally motivated to do good work and accomplish high levels of productivity." They include:

- Active goal setting

- Understanding how their role fits into the big picture

- Determination

- Persistence

- Participation in professional development

- Willingness to learn new things

- Positive approach to challenges

- Task initiation rather than acceptance

- Providing a positive influence in the workplace

Questions that you may ask your employer regarding these examples may be:

How does my position fit into the larger scale of things within the company?

Finding out where you are going to fit in the organizational structure is important. If you will be working for a newspaper and you are going to play a communicative role, this is a huge responsibility. Being the "middle man" at that type of an organization is imperative for the company to operate. You want to be sure of whom you will be reporting to and who in turn will be reporting to you.

Do you feel that my level of determination fits into the role I am interviewing for?

Again, you can turn the tables on the interviewer. Does she think you are suitable for the position? This is a good question to ask when you want to check your progress throughout the interview.

Will I have to consistently report to upper management, or am I going to be able to initiate work on my own?

I am a team player and I love to be involved in the workplace. Are there any organizations that I will be able to participate in, such as self-help or international awareness groups?

Are all signs pointing toward "yes" in your interview? Do you feel as if the position is challenging yet rewarding at the same time? Are you getting excited just thinking about being offered the position? Then this company might be a match!

It is always exciting to take on a position that keeps you feeling upbeat. You want to look for something that fills a void within yourself. If you are a nurturer, find a career path that is going to help you fulfill that need. Do you enjoy the outdoors? Why not look into jobs that require you to be outside for a substantial part of the day? Keep yourself in mind first, and then look for the position you want to try to tackle.

Upon being hired, what types of assignments will I be given?

Here is where you are able to see directly into the tasks that the company is going to hand you. You are able to find the majority of things that you might be doing on a daily basis. If the answer is something that you think sounds interesting, then this might just be a match.

Is there any other positions that this job usually leads to within the company?

This gives the employer a chance to describe where you could end up with hard work and determination. It then gives you a chance to evaluate his or her answer and see if this is a fit. Do you want to end up where they are describing? Be sure to listen attentively to the answer being provided.

Recent Graduates

Podormoff stated, "When dealing with a recent graduate that has little previous work experience, the answers to the behavioral questions will come from educational experiences. It is important to understand his or her educational experience and the context in which he or she learned and performed well, and not so well. Although work is different than school, it still requires most of the same competencies: communication, teamwork, motivation, initiative, organization, etc."

During my studies, I heard from three recent college graduates. Every one of them was nervous going into their initial interviews. School and work are not the same thing. However, if you have a good work ethic in your studies, then chances are you will bring that over into your work environment. All of the graduates said that an internship was a major benefit to them when starting out their careers.

William Ronald says, "What are your suggestions for someone who is trying to find a career in your line of work? Complete at least one major internship to get your foot in the door. There are many positions out there, but the community is very small. It will not be too difficult to make a good name for yourself as a pro-active hard worker. On the other hand, you can also make a bad name for yourself easily.

Weslty Kuer expresses similar thoughts. He says, "Find an internship with a sports franchise/facility that you would like to work for one day. Many companies hire within, as an intern, you will stand out to a GM or president if you do a good job and will have a great chance to turn that internship into a full-time position."

Kristi Wehe was asked, "What brought you to the position you hold today?" She answered, "Careful thought about my skills, previous positions I had held, and what I felt would ultimately suit me. I asked myself about things like what I wanted from my career, what I needed in terms of money, etc."

When asked, "Where do you suggest someone go when looking for a career?," William Ronald and Westly Kuer both gave their advice: "Nowadays the internet is probably the best source for an employee looking for a career. Most industries have specific Web sites that list only jobs in the field that the employee is looking for. They can search using specific criteria. Most of these are pay services, but it is worth it because employers are more likely to post there job there. College career fairs are a great place for entry-level employees to network and see professionals in all different types of careers.

7

Advancement

Knowing where the position you are interviewing for might lead you may help you through this difficult process. Make sure there is room for you to grow within the organization. During the interview, ask questions that lead to answers pertaining to information that can show you into the future. Most structures have a demand chain. Do you agree with their structure? If you are able to achieve all the goals that you set for yourself and you always go beyond, will you be promoted? Make sure to fit these types of questions into your interview. It is important to find out if there is room to grow within the organization.

Who wants to be stuck in a position that has no growth potential? Asking questions helps you see what your future might hold within this company. Ask for examples of success stories within the organization. People tend to enjoy sharing these types of stories during interviews. It gives employers a chance to reflect positively on the past. Everyone tends to enjoy reflecting on positive experiences, so go ahead and speak up. They will let you in on these aspects of the organization, but only if you ask.

Make sure to ask yourself what answers you are looking for before the interview. If you see yourself at the top of the demand chain in the next few years, you need find out at the interview if this is attainable. While asking questions, be sure to listen for clues. Did the interviewer give you any examples pertaining to someone advancing to the top in just a few years? If so, feel confident that this could happen to you. Alternatively, has the employer been at the company for 25 years without any sort of advancement? This may be a warning sign for you. It is always important to consider these things.

Podmoroff offers this information: "Often initiative is born out of necessity, and while the average employee will sit back and let the boss deal with problems down the road, the employee who is driven and sees the big picture will recognize the opportunity and devise a plan to address it. What you want to know is how successfully the candidate developed a proactive solution to a problem before it even became a problem. Candidates who provide solid answers to these types of questions deserve serious consideration; however, recognize that not all interviewees will be able to come up with appropriate or relevant answers. Work with what you get and make the best evaluation you can."

Show the employer that you are willing and able to take initiative consistently. Describe to the interviewer examples of when you took initiative while you were holding your previous position. You can also use examples of your family life. Most people who take initiative during their personal lives also do so at work. Let you employer know that you take leadership seriously and keep them informed about the many tasks you take on daily.

Progress

Progress depends on how far you are willing to go to impress your employer. Are you a hard worker? Do you always try to go beyond the duties asked of you? Have you always been dedicated to progress? If the answer to all these questions is "yes," then you are golden. Hard work does pay off in the end. You want to make this clear to the employer by giving examples of how you have previously achieved promotions. Maybe you are excellent with customer service. Did this lead to advancement at your former place of employment? Do not be afraid to share this during the interviewing process. Companies want to hear success stories. They can bring your stories to the table while deliberating on whom they should hire for the position.

How far will you go to receive a promotion? During the interview process, you should make your efforts clear. You should ask questions pertaining to what the company expects of its employees in order for them to advance. This is your chance to find out whom you are going to have to impress, as well as how much work needs to be done in order to grab a hold of a higher position within the organization.

Besides hard work, what else are you looking for in the lines of advancement?

This question gives the employer a chance to reflect on past experiences. The answer to this question betters your chances for advancement in the future. Take note of these answers. This is sort of a cheat question for the future. You will not only learn about past experiences, but also about your future endeavors.

Does this organization have branches elsewhere that I could look into later for advancement opportunities?

When you are applying to an organization that has multiple branches this might be a great question to ask. Say you do not have a family and are able to move every few years. This can be a great way to obtain information on other organizations that your current prospect may lead you toward.

Travel within an organization can be a benefit. A larger company may present you with plenty of travel opportunities. Some organizations even pay your expenses. All of this information is imperative when considering your employment with a company.

If I am hired and I perform well, what other opportunities might this job lead to?

Here is where the employer may elaborate on other positions within the organization that you may fit into after hard work and dedication. Listen up and take note of these opportunities.

If I do a good job, where do you see me in the next year?

If you are looking to advance within a corporation, this is a logical question to ask. This question gives you the answer to how quickly a person can move through the ranks at this particular organization. You may want to ask questions that are more specific. One may be.

Can you give me an example of someone who quickly rose to upper management?

This question gives the employer a chance to elaborate on what, whom, and when a specific person's advancement took place. It helps you understand how the organization treats those employees who have a positive influence within the organization.

Expectations

Podmoroff gives us a few pointers on what the employer is looking for in the interviewee's personality; the interviewer's job is to assess the following:

Ability to follow established guidelines.

Are you able to follow instructions in full without having to continuously ask questions? Let the interviewer know that you enjoy taking initiative and have no problem following guidelines.

Understanding and respect for policies and procedures.

Give the interviewers examples of how you are able to follow rules and guidelines. Make them aware that you have no problem conforming to the organization's policies and procedures.

Recognition of the importance of consistency.

Show the employer that you are able to recognize the importance of doing things right the first time and on a consistent basis. Let the interviewer know about tasks you have previously done on a dependable basis. Give the employer examples of how you feel that consistency is important and relevant in the workplace.

Level of impulsive behavior.

As the interviewer asks you questions relating to impulsive behavior illustrate that you feel comfortable with your impulses and enjoy acting upon them. If you have an example of when you acted upon an impulse and it worked out in your favor, feel free to share it during this portion of your interview.

Ability to stick to a routine.

Let the employer know that you are able to stick to a daily routine. During this part of the interview, give examples of your routine during work or everyday life.

This shows the employer that you are aware that routine conditions a person and gives them a sense of purpose.

Here, Podmoroff lists leadership questions. These questions focus on the following characteristics:

• Open and accessible communicator

• Team player

- Values diversity

- Fosters creativity

- Shares information and expectations

- Welcomes ideas

- Values all contributions

- Facilitates participation

- Acknowledges mistakes

- Demonstrates enthusiasm

- Offers feedback

- Acts as a role model

- Empowers others

The interviewer is going to focus on the above characteristics. Come to the interview prepared to demonstrate your skills in these particular areas. Show the interviewer that you are an open communicator. You may share personal stories about yourself or just answer questions extremely honestly. Make it known that you welcome all conversation and that you enjoy communicating openly with others.

As we talked about earlier employers want someone who is willing to work in a team. Keep yourself positive and let the employers know your feelings about teamwork. Prove that you are a team player by giving examples of when you have previously worked in teams and have had positive outcomes.

When I worked in an advertising team, we all had our individual roles and responsibilities. In order to keep everything straight we would all meet once aweek to make sure everyone was on the same track. I initiated these meetings because after awhile I realized that some of the same tasks were being done twice. This essentially was a waste of time. Therefore, I took things into my own hands in order to eliminate confusion.

This proved to work well for my team. Everyone works differently so you need to keep everyone on the same page. Employers like to hear stories such as this one. It proves that you have initiative and the ability to lead others. Not all employers like to constantly monitor their staff. Show you can motivate your coworkers.

Employers value diversity and this plays into teamwork. When working in teams we are often among diverse groups of people. Are you open to diversity? Express your values in terms of how they affect diversity.

Are you a creative person? Do you use your creativity to help you within the workplace? What types of examples can you share with your interviewer? You may want to ask your employer if they are open to creativity. Say something along the lines of,

Does your workplace openly welcome creativity during work assignments?

The answer to this question may help you decide if you want to work at this organization. Most organizations welcome creativity, but you want to know where the organization stands on all issues before you decide to be employed by them.

The employer is going to ask you about your expectations of employment with their particular company. Be open and honest when answering these types of questions. That being said, it is important to be realistic as well. Share with the employer what you would expect during your employment with them. Your expectations are important to the employer. They want to see what they can expect from you as well. This is why you need to be prepared with your expectations.

Where do you see yourself in five years? Employers are likely to ask you this question during the interview process. Answers vary across the board. Let the employer know that you want to advance within the organization. Do not hesitate to be honest in regards to making your way to the top. Keep you answer positive and upbeat. Give them the sense that you are "in it to win it."

During the process, the interviewer is going to ask you questions that help them see if you are open to new ideas. Depending on what they ask you, you need to be able to listen attentively to their questions and answer accordingly. Why are they asking you this particular question? What type of answer do you feel they are looking for? If you are unsure or uncomfortable with the question, there is no harm in asking, "Why are you they asking you this particular question?" Your questions are just as important as theirs are.

Are you open to new ideas? How can you express this to the employer? Take all of this into consideration.

Contribution

Do other people's opinions matter to you? I hope that they do because most organizations consist of group environments. Everyone is contributing to the company in one form or another. From the janitor to the delivery person all roles serve their purposes. When I worked at Lakeland Square Mall, I quickly struck up a friendship with the janitor. He was a humble man with an amazing work ethic. After just a few short months, I learned a lesson that I will take with me for the rest of my life.

I no longer leave misplaced trash in public places. Before meeting him, sometimes I would aim and miss the trashcan. After doing so, I would turn away and go on my way. Now, after having a personal relationship with someone who had to pick that misplaced garbage, I see my littering from a different point of view.

This helped me to see just how important the janitor's role is at the workplace. People are constantly leaving trash around. Without the janitorial role, companies would be altogether filthy. It would make it much more difficult to work and be efficient. Each person and his or her position make the organization function. Make the employer know that you understand this and appreciate others no matter what their role.

Your willingness to contribute to the organization is important to the employer. "What types of groups within the company are there that I can get involved with?" These questions show the employer that you are eager to join the organization and contribute your ideas and abilities.

As a representative of XYZ Company, what do you feel is the most important contribution this company expects from its employees?

Here is a question to help you figure out the job duties as well as the moral aspects of the company. This gives you an idea of what the employer expects of you, as well as where they stand in the overall process.

When asked, "Who has influenced you the most in your career?" Craig Fowler replied, "My family. I have been married for more than 12 years, and have two wonderful children (with one on the way). My wife is extremely supportive of my travels and late nights, and my kids are a joy. I live for them on the weekends. My wife is my biggest cheerleader and my fairest critic."

Joseph McCormack stated, "What brought me to the position I hold today, which is Managing Partner of McCormack & Associates, a retain executive search firm? I entered the search business in 1976, after five years as a staff member for the Young Presidents' Organization, with the intention of starting my own practice. I spent my first five years learning the business from large search firms in New York and Los Angeles, and launched my first venture with Jerry Farrow in 1982. McCormack & Farrow is now the largest retained search practice based in Orange County, California. I sold my interest in that firm to found McCormack & Associates in Los Angeles in 1993.

These men's insight can give us a lot of guidance. Learning how someone has used circumstances to rise to the top is not only amazing but also motivational and inspiring. You can learn from others' experiences, and you should use these experiences as a benefit during job searches.

Do not be overly confident. No one wants to hire someone who is too self-involved, and therefore feels that he or she is never wrong. Let the employer know that you have made mistakes in the past. This does not mean that you are a bad employee. Tell the employer about a particular mistake you have made, and then let him or her know how you managed to repair that slip-up.

A part of being human is making mistakes. Employers cannot expect perfection. Instead, they want to hire someone who is able to recognize his or her mistakes, and fix them in a timely manner. This is someone who is effective in the workplace.

Are you an enthused individual? When you looked into this position, did you get excited? Tell the employer this. No one wants to hire someone who is not interested in what he is doing. It is important to be enthusiastic about your work. Let the employer know that the objectives excite you, and you are more than willing to tackle all obstacles that stand in your way. People want to hire others who are excited about what they do. So show your enthusiasm. Do not be afraid to let the employer know that this job excites you, and that is why you are here today.

Let the employer know how you feel about the position, and how the interview is going. If you do not comment on what you are feeling, then you are not being honest. People want feedback during conversations and although this is not exactly a conversation, you need to be prepared to give feedback to all questions asked of you.

Are you a role model? Who looks up to you? Give the employer examples of whom you have affected during your professional years. If you were previously a manager and had a few employees under you who always asked for your advice, tell the employer this.

Consider who you look up to. Everyone seems to get inspiration from different sources. An interview with Ken Sundheim mirrors this philosophy. When asked, "Who has influenced you the most in your career?" Sundheim said, "My wife, Alison. Ali also works at KAS Placement. She left her job in public relations and came to work with me about eight months after starting KAS Placement. She is someone in the business whom I can be honest with, bounce ideas off of and rely on to give 100 percent of her efforts on every project. Most business owners do not have the luxury of getting an honest opinion from their co-workers or subordinates; if it wasn't for my wife, I would not have had the success I've enjoyed."

The empowerment of others is something that the employer looks for from his or her employees. Do not neglect to tell the employer about your admiration of others throughout your working years. This is a sign that you are a humble individual and that other people give you inspiration.

Creativity is not limited to artistic people. Creativity is a person's ability to generate creative or original solutions to problems, and find innovative ways to solve old problems. Creativity is a valuable competency because it demonstrates an ability to think beyond a job description, and see how a role affects coworkers, supervisors, and the overall performance of the company.

What Podmoroff is saying here is that employers are looking for someone who is creative with his or her work. Everyday work life can sometimes get monotonous, and employers are looking for candidates who bring differences with them into the workplace. Try to show the employer that you are creative in your ways of thinking and in your ways of going about things. Have you ever made a difference by thinking outside the box? Employers are impressed with these kinds of examples.

Give the employer reasons to hire you. Organizations do not want to hire executives who are exactly alike. Be proud of your differences, and let the employers know how you can use your differences to their benefit. Provide examples of your abilities and how you can use them to the company's betterment during your interview. Let the employer know that you are willing to share your sense of creativity.

8

Why Me?

Hiring From Within

Why is this company looking to you for this position? This is an important question to ask yourself and the employer. Do you feel that they are looking outside the company to fill this position? If so, then why? Does everyone within the organization avoid the available positions? Are they only looking to you because they have run out of options? You want to ask these questions and more. No one wants to be the last resort.

There are many reasons for hiring someone outside of an organization. It is important to get different perspectives. Fresh blood comes with fresh ideas. A company that never lets anyone in from the outside risks being stuck in a rut. You want to make sure of the reasons the company is looking to you. Get the organization to prove to you that their reasons are legit and beneficial to everyone involved.

Do you have the proper job experience to obtain this position? Chances are you do or you would not have made it through the door. Use this to your advantage. Everyone tends to be nervous during an interview but make sure that you let the employer know you are self-aware. Be confident in the skills you have already acquired. Feel free to share these skills during the discussion. You have made it this far for a reason. The interview process is draining on everyone so do not let it get you down.

Stay confident and let the employer know that you are present with the skills, as well as the ability to conquer this position. This is just the company's chance to get to know you better.

I know that, for the position with which I am interviewing, the company decided to recruit from outside the organization. How did you decide between recruiting from within and going outside?

The answer to this question lies within the interviewer. This might throw the interviewer off. There are always reasons behind hiring from outside the organization. It is hugely important to know why this position has opened up and why someone from within is not able to cover this position. Is this a position that takes certain skills that most people do not have?

Alternatively, is this position commonly filled repeatedly because there is something lacking with it? If the answer is the later, you may want to look elsewhere. You do not want to get into a position that has a high turnover rate. Chances are the rate is high for good reason.

Skills and Abilities

When Clark was asked; "What do you feel is the most important question in a job interview?" His response was as follows:

"The most important question asked in a job interview is, 'Why do you want this job?' It sets the direction for the rest of the interview. If the answer focuses primarily on the money, title or location, the interview will be short in length. If the response deals with interests, motivation and values of the candidate, it will strike a more positive note and set the right tone for what is to follow."

Clark describes the importance of answering the above question with poise and direction. You want to show the interviewer that you are in fact interested in the position. Also, the interviewer wants to see that you are in this for the correct reasons. So take note when tackling these difficult questions. Be aware that the interviewer is looking for the correct response and not just any response. Your answers affect the pace and length of the interview.

Ken Sundheim was asked about suggestions for someone trying to find a career in his line of work. His answer was as follows: "Similar to any field, you must be cautious of the type of employment agency you choose. Some recruiting firms are great and are full of intelligent, successful people. However, because there is a low entry bar and minimal base salary, many firms are not selective about their employee pool and are unpleasant places to work. They often see their success and financial resources quickly drained.

When entering the field, it is best to begin with a specialty and get very good at it. You have to think to yourself, "Do I want to be in law recruitment, sales recruitment, technology recruitment or some other facet?" You should go with what interests you. If you do not like computers, stay away from IT recruiting firms."

I would also suggest reading a book on recruiting. Being a headhunter is not for everyone. In most cases, there is no steady paycheck, as most firms provide health insurance and pay on commission; you must prepare yourself for that. Be aware that this business is very competitive and economically sensitive. When the times are good, they are great and when corporate hiring slows, it seems as if the office is a ghost town. Get to know the lay of the land as well as the ups and downs before diving into recruitment."

How do my skills compare with those of the other candidates you have interviewed?

You want to leave this question for the end of the interview, or even wait for the second or final interview. It is a powerful question that will let you know exactly where you stand. It also puts the interviewer on the spot, and gives you a direct view of where you fit in their minds. Be prepared for honest feedback. The answer will give you insight as to what the company most highly regards.

Here are Podmoroff's feelings about interviewing: "Interviewing at its best is a structured conversation. The interviewer is in control of how the conversation will flow, and the interviewee determines the actual content of the conversation through his or her responses to questions and probes. An ineffective interview is one that deteriorates into an impromptu conversation. While having a good ol' chat with someone is a way to pass the time, it is not going to reveal anything other than what the interviewee wants to reveal usually a false impression. Basing hiring decisions on a "gut feel" approach is the most common source of grievous hiring mistakes, and this approach needs to be avoided at all costs.

Throughout the getting-to-know-you phase of the interview, be aware of the applicant's poise, style of delivery and communication ability; these are all valuable clues to whether or not the person is suitable for the job and whether he or she will fit into the work environment."

In this excerpt, Podmoroff is giving us the interviewer's perspective. This is important to the interviewee because, if we know where the interviewer is coming from, we may be able to give them what they are looking for and therefore get an offer. Note that the interviewee determines the conversation. So make sure that you lead the employer to discuss your best attributes. If you are wary of certain areas in the field, try to avoid them by speaking about areas you feel most comfortable in. There are always ways to lead the conversation in your favor.

In addition, Podmoroff states that the interviewer is noting your poise, style, delivery, and communication ability. These are all things we need to consider before walking into the interview. Make yourself confident by wearing the appropriate attire. Not only will you look your best, but you will feel your best as well. If you feel your best, you tend to hold yourself in an interview appropriate manner. This includes standing straight and tall, and not fidgeting. When you are fidgety, it makes everyone aware that you are feeling nervous and you are not self-aware. This is something that the interviewee should avoid.

So, take a deep breath and walk into the interview with your head held high. Be confident in your answers. Speak freely and with determination. Do not let the employer see that you are nervous. Make sure that you project your voice toward everyone in the room. This shows that you are self-aware and does not leave people questioning your abilities to address a group.

Previous Employment

People have many reasons for leaving different places of work. Everyone has a past hence the reason for a resume. An interviewer is probably going to ask you about where you previously worked. So be prepared for questions pertaining to dates and why and when you left the place of your most previous employment.

Podormoff writes, "The main purpose for asking these questions are to get the candidate comfortable talking about their previous positions. You get information that goes beyond the traditional résumé list of responsibilities, giving you insight into the context of prior work. Gaining a better understanding of the person's prior work will help enormously when trying to make sense of the answers given to the behavioral questions."

Therefore, when you feel as if your employer is asking you questions that related to your previous employer do not feel that they are probing unnecessarily. They may just be trying to get you comfortable with the subject matter before moving on to something else. With this in mind you should prepare accordingly. Go over your résumé and refresh your memory on dates and reason for leaving previous positions.

Problems

Organizational Problems

All organizations have their problems just as individual businesses have their hardships. You want to be well aware of these hardships before you begin a position with the company. There is no harm in inquiring about the problems the organization is facing during the interview. This shows a sign of interest as well as a concern for the structure of the company. Knowing where the company needs improvement can give you an edge over the competition. If you can make a suggestion or let the employer, know you are capable of fixing the problem during the interview, this will put you a step ahead of your competitors. There is no way of knowing unless you ask questions about the company's hardships and concerns.

If the employer gives you examples of where the company needs improvement, this gives you an idea of whether or not the position is right for you. If a company knows where it is weak, this shows you that the organization is aware that there is room for improvement. You do not want to work for an arrogant corporation. Just as you would not want to date someone in your personal life that is arrogant, you do not want to work for an organization that thinks they cannot stand to improve a few things.

Be wary if a company tells you that they do not see any room for improvement. An employer may throw this question back your way so be sure to do some research before you ask these types of questions. Make certain that you can list a few things you see that may be difficulties for the organization at hand. If the employer turns the questions back your way, it is important to be prepared. Use examples that you can suggest positive answers to. This shows that you have done your homework and that you keep the organization's best interests at heart.

Are there any problems or situations that I should be aware of that the position is facing at this time?

Because the company is hiring someone for this current position there is probably a problem or a situation involved as to why they need someone to fill this position. The answer to this question may bring you insight as to what types of duties you will be performing on a daily basis, as well as how to approach the rest of the interview.

Podmoroff goes on to explain her thoughts on stress: "Stress and pressure are in abundance in today's workplace, and the presence of either often brings out employees' worst behaviors, habits, and attitudes. Some stress is motivating, yet too much stress can be debilitating, not to mention a serious health concern. What you, as the interviewer, need to assess is whether the candidate has developed mechanisms to cope with stress and whether the strategies are successful."

Weaknesses

When speaking about your weaknesses, be sure to provide either a weakness within yourself that can be seen as a strength, or use a weakness that you are diligently working on improving. Give examples of how you are overcoming that weakness on a daily basis. When employers ask this question, they are striving to find out what makes you tick. They want to know if you are self-motivated and willing to take things into your own hands and fix them without too much coaching from others. An example of a weakness that could be considered a strength is being a workaholic. Some people might not see this as a weakness so try to research the organization, and see what types of employees it already has. See how you can turn your weakness around in and put a positive spin on it.

What do you consider the organization's strengths and weaknesses?

This is a counter question to something that the employer may or may not ask you. Asking this question gives you an idea on what types of struggles the company is dealing with. This gives you a time to shine if you can suggest something from an outsider prospective that may help the organization overcome its weaknesses. It also lets you know what areas the company's executives feel the company is excelling in. If what the company is doing well interests you and you feel that it is beneficial, this company may be a match.

When the employer starts to press about pressures in the workplace and stress related questions, give them positive feedback. Let the interviewer know that you are capable of handling stress. Give them responses that include your ability to work under pressure. Also let them see that everyday work pressures are expected. Show them that you are able to handle these stresses without letting them get to you.

Podmoroff list some of the more common stress-management tools to be aware of include:

- Identifying stress triggers

- Eliminating stressors

- Reducing the intensity of emotional reactions to stress

- Moderating physical reactions to stress

• Building physical reserves

• Maintaining emotional reserves

Ask the employer the expected stresses are in the position you are interviewing for.

What do you recommend I do to eliminate some of the more common stressors during the day?

Here the interviewer may give you some examples of what he or she does to reduce stress.

Do you have any examples of what employees usually do to reduce stress?

This question lets you in on the level of tension that may arise in this work environment. Maybe there is a break room she can show you or an exercise facility. Everyone release stress in a different way. Examples are always great for ideas.

Are there any physical aliments you have recognized your employees have related to this position's stress?

Stress can cause serious illness and if an organization has extremely stressed out employees you should be wary. The answer "no" is best here. If the environment is causing peoples health to decline, flee the scene!

Have you witnessed employees being able to maintain emotional reserves?

Podmoroff stresses, "Be aware that most people know what they should do to manage stress in their lives; your job is to determine if they actually can and do manage it."

The employer is looking to you to provide them with an ease about your emotional state. This can be done by keeping your anxiety at the interview to a minimum. As stressed earlier, try to keep fidgeting to a minimum. If you feel that the stress of the interview is getting to you, take a deep breath, relax, and remember you are here to evaluate the employer as well as to have the employer evaluate you.

This in turn may open up the door for you to inquire about the organization's weaknesses. You want to make sure that there is not a weakness within the organization that is impossible to overcome. Organizations all have their strong points, but they also all have their weak points as well. Try to decipher what their weaknesses are. Maybe you can help them overcome these things. Do you have any suggestions that might help them get out of a hole? Let the employer know that you are interested in helping them out of the situation they find themselves in.

Podmoroff describes the interview as "intimidating for all parties." The interviewer wants to present a positive image of the company, and the interviewee wants to present his or her "best self" in hopes of being offered the job. This nervous tension provides the perfect environment for false impressions and social niceties when what you need in an interview is a real conversation with a real person. That way both parties can assess whether or not there is a good fit and how likely it is that an employment relationship will be successful."

Make sure that you do yourself, as well as the employer, a favor and be your real "best self." Everyone has been known to fake it every once in awhile. During the interviewing process, you do not want to "fake it." Show your "best self" by demonstrating your real abilities. Do not demonstrate abilities that are not your own. If you do this, you will be caught in the end. Whether it is a few days or a few months from now, you do not want to be caught with your hands in the cookie jar. If an employer asks you about an ability that you do not have, simply let them know that you do not have that particular ability right now. Let them know though that you are more than happy to try to acquire that skill.

Podmoroff describes the ability to solve problems like so: "The ability to solve problems is a skill that oftentimes goes unrecognized. People who are good at solving problems often do so at an almost subconscious level. Your role in the interview is to draw out the automatic process that a candidate goes through when solving a problem and then evaluate the overall effectiveness of the approach."

If you are aware before the interview that the employer is going to be asking you to solve problems, think ahead and get prepared with suitable answers. As Podmoroff says, the interviewer is testing your problem solving skills. Show the employer that you are a strategic thinker and you are able to squash problems quickly and effectively. When approaching the interview, prepare by giving yourself examples to problems that might come up during a regular workday in the particular field in which you are interviewing. Test yourself by giving multiple answers to a specific problem. This gets you in the proper mindset and keeps you feeling confident.

Podmoroff goes on to say, "The purpose of questions regarding a person's analytical ability is to uncover how well the candidate can gather information and extract relevant data. Today's workplaces are rife with information overload, so it is imperative that employees be able to make sense of and analyze vast amounts of information efficiently and accurately. Whether reaching conclusions, solving problems or making valid decisions, a productive employee needs strong analytical skills."

The interviewer is going to test your analytical skills during the interview process. This means that he or she will be analyzing whether or not you are able to handle information overload. Give the interviewer examples of when you have used your multitasking abilities to the benefit of your previous employer. Whether you finished a research project while answering phones or gave a presentation totally on your own while passing out all pamphlets and answering questions, show the interviewer that you can process and analyze all types of information at once. Everyone wants to hire someone who is capable of multitasking. It is imperative that you are able to do more than one task at a time and have a completed project that looks like it had your undivided attention.

When the interviewer asks about certain ability that you do not possess, do not be afraid to let them know that you do not possess that characteristic. An employer would rather hire a humble person that does not possess a certain skill than someone who lies about his or her abilities. By lying to an employer, you are putting pressure on yourself, as well as being dishonest. If you are straightforward with the employer, they are more likely to hire you. No one is perfect, and employers do not expect you to be. So go ahead and show your "best self"; just be wary of stepping into someone else's "best self."

Some might say that you are putting your job in jeopardy here but honesty is the best policy. If you are unable to do one of the many tasks that are required of you and the employer chooses someone else over you because of something mundane, then you are better off elsewhere anyway. Do not let this get you flustered. In my experience, I have found that employers enjoy your honesty.

Give them examples of how you are highly coach able and willing to take on any challenge. Prove to them that you have conquered tasks at your previous places of employment that you never thought you were capable of.

When I signed on to be a graphic artist I had never done anything of the sort. I was asked if I possessed the skills and I let the employer know that I did not. The interviewer was a bit shocked but the rest of the interview went really well. I expressed that though I did not have the skills at the time, that I was more than willing to learn them. I did however possess all of the other skills that were required for the position. I ended up being offered a similar position.

While I was at the place of employment, I was trained on the advance equipment that I had never touched. I was then able to do the work that I had previously interviewed for. Now I possess a skill that I can use for the rest of my life. If I had strayed from the interview because of my lack of knowledge of the exact programs I would never had not been offered the job, nor would I be able to do graphic work to this day. So do not be afraid to give it to them straight. Not everyone possesses every skill. Show that you are able to take on any tasks and the position might be yours regardless of your one small flaw.

10

What Have I Left Out?

Questions

When the interview is getting close to an end, make certain to ask yourself, "What have I left out?" This helps you go over in your head all the questions that you wanted to ask this employer. Did you find out salary information? Are there going to be health benefits? Do you feel as if you can conquer this position? Try not to leave the interview without getting all your questions answered.

If you are feeling comfortable with all your questions, you might want to ask the interviewer if they feel you have left something out. This gives the employer a chance to go over his or her information, and ask any questions that he or she might have missed. Asking this question lets the interviewer know that you are aware that he or she is trying to obtain a goal during this process. It shows that you respect the process, and realize it is not all just up to you. This is a difficult process for him or her as well.

Clark answers the following question: "Have you ever witnessed a perfect interview?

"I don't believe there is such a thing. While I have often finished an interview thinking, 'that went really well,' typically there is a question I forgot to ask or a topic I should have delved into further. I do think it is good advice for candidates and interviewers to make sure that those forgotten questions don't get dropped. From the candidate's perspective it is a good way to follow up after the interview."

Here Clark is describing that both the interviewer and the interviewee sometimes forget to ask certain questions. So this part of the interview is helpful to both parties. Do not hesitate to ask questions at this point. It is your chance to gain the insight that you see fit. There are certain risks that you must take in order to find out what fits your needs. Keep yourself ahead of the game by not shying away from questions that you see difficult to ask. You will thank yourself later.

Concerns

Before I leave, do you have any other concerns regarding my ability to conquer this position?

Asking this question lets the interviewer know that you are confident and not afraid of any further questions. It lets them know that you are excited to take on the task and want to prove that you are the correct candidate for the position.

Show the employer that you want to use this time wisely. It is important for you to lay everything on the table in order for them to make the correct decision. You do not want to waste their time as well as your own. This interview is important to both parties involved; let them know that you realize that.

Are there any answers to questions I gave you that you felt were too vague?

Here you are letting the employer take time to reevaluate your answers and give you honest feedback. Maybe they felt that you did not satisfy all aspects of the question. This is their chance to go over that question again with you. This question helps you and the employer.

Is there anything else that you feel you want to go over?

By asking this question, you are letting the employer take a step back and look over his or her questions one more time. They might have left out one question that is essential in the interviewing process. You are showing your confidence by approaching the interviewer with this type of question.

According to Podmoroff, "The whole idea of interviewing is that it is a structured conversation. The structure comes from standard questions; the conversation element relies on a natural flow of questions and answers. If the candidate is heading in the wrong direction, reel him or her in; if the candidate heads into a different direction than expected, evaluate the usefulness of the information and proceed as appropriate. No information is bad information; your job is to extract the most relevant information, and if a candidate offers something that is potentially beneficial, you need to be flexible enough to capitalize on the situation."

"Remain flexible throughout the interview and be open to probing for information outside the competency being investigated."

Here Podmoroff is explaining the interviewer is trying to stay on task during the interview. You should take note of this. Try to stay on course yourself. Answer only the questions asked and do not offer any irrelevant information. Be careful not to over share. It is not harmful to your interview if you share information that is beneficial to you, but try to keep the information shared relevant to the conversation at hand. Do not go off on a tangent about something positive you accomplished at your previous organization if the interviewer is asking you questions about something to the contrary. Keep the side conversations to a minimum. Show the employer that you are interested in what they are discussing. Let them know that you are listening by answering them with concise answers to the questions at hand.

"What does it take to become a member of your organization?"

Here are a few examples of answers to this question from our case studies.

Kristie Wehe of Weststaff; "Depends on what position you are looking for. Generally speaking, we are looking for professional people with a passion for the industry."

William Ronald: "Must possess a knowledge of sports, this includes the rules, regulations and play of particular sports. You must be able to plan organize and direct events. Marketing of events is a daily task."

Ken Sundheim; "When I hire employees, I look for a few must-haves. If any of these traits or skills is not present, I pass. First, it is a must that everyone whom I work with (or works at my company) has very strong writing and verbal skills. In my line of work, you have to be able to effectively work with and gain the respect of many different types of people. In business, people only follow and respect those can quickly and consistently demonstrate their intelligence.

They must also have a friendly, caring personality. I began KAS Placement on the premise that we would be different from other companies. Instead of seeing an applicant as a quick buck, I make sure to care about the needs of the people with whom we work. The same is expected from everyone at my company. As a headhunter, if all you care about is the money an applicant can generate, it will be apparent to your candidates and sour your reputation.

I also need everybody in the office to be able to use his or her intelligence to its fullest extent. I want people who want to make a difference in my company. When I hire someone, I do not just hire him or her for his or her recruiting skills. I want someone who has a drive to make the company better. I want to see them act as if they owned KAS Placement themselves."

Benefits

Benefits are a huge bonus when looking into a corporation. A lot of businesses push the fact that they have a well equipped compensation package. These days, benefits are almost a must when looking into employment. If a company is without benefits you need to consider this strongly. Company perks such as benefits can way heavily in the decisions making process. Finding out about benefits during the interviewing process is essential.

Studies say that asking about a company's benefits during the first interview makes you look needy and resistible. That said, make sure not to come off distastefully. However, you also want to ensure that the company is well-equipped with a benefits package. Usually, an organization goes over benefits during the interview process as a form of reeling you in. However, if this is not the case in your particular interview, then feel free to inquire about what the company offers. Just be sure to use a tasteful approach.

After all, this is something that is going to affect your job, well being, and family. Sometimes you might accept a lower salary if the right benefit package is involved. So inquiring about whether or not there are benefits, and or what the benefits might be is pertinent. Keep this in mind throughout the interview process.

11

Guidance

Regardless of how an interview is going you can always take something from it. When it is your turn to ask the questions make sure to consider gaining guidance from those in the room with you. You may want to ask for advice or leadership on an issue. This is a time to sit back and learn from someone in the field of work you are looking into. Some questions may be:

Advice

"What types of advice would you give someone in my position?"

Here you are inquiring about the individual that is interviewing you. It is always beneficial to sit back and listen to an outsider's point of view. Everyone may have a different opinion about what you should do, but it always helps to consider all options. You never know; they may suggest the exact thing that will help you succeed.

"What have you learned from holding your position with this organization?"

The interviewer is going to be able to share what he or she has learned during their time within the particular organization. This is extremely beneficial to you in your decision making process. Hearing what others have achieved and accomplished through the years is going to give you insight into whether or not this position is right for you.

The answers to these questions and more can guide you in the resolution that lies ahead.

In every experience, there is a lesson to be learned. I realized this when looking for a job myself. After graduating with a degree in communications, I was not sure what I wanted to do with my life. I knew that I needed a position, but I was not sure where my passion was. The interesting thing was that I did extremely well on interviews, but I was having a hard time finding exactly what I wanted. I would go to interviews and find out details of the organization that did not fit with my personality. Their goals were not the same as mine or I did not find the structural aspect of the company to be appealing. This led me to other opportunities, though. You will not learn anything from sitting home. So get out there and start interviewing. Eventually, you will find a match, depending on what your passion is.

Even if you are unlike myself and know exactly what you want to do, there are questions to be asked. You may find that your dream organization and position is not all it was cracked up to be. This is something that is better to find out during your interview than a few months into employment. If you find yourself second-guessing the position during your interview, then do not take the job. Even if there are great benefits and good pay, if you do not believe in the common goal you will be working toward, it is not worth it.

People have choices and your choices are endless if you are willing to put the effort into it.

Do not let yourself get so sucked into the interview process that you forget to take something away from it for yourself. Just because others are questioning you does not mean that you cannot turn the tables. Use this process to your advantage.

Experience

Is this position something you have done before?

If the answer is "yes" then you can feel comfortable with their abilities to train you properly. When someone has not actually taken on the responsibilities, which you are working toward it makes them less suitable to do the training. So be aware of who will be training you and what their capabilities are.

I have unfortunately had an experience where my hiring manager oversaw my training. She was a very intelligent woman but just had no experience training anyone. Therefore, she reluctantly left me "in the dust" so to speak. Even though I muddied my way through there were some tuff lessons for both of us along the way. So, if you are up for the challenge go for it, but if you are already considerably busy with the rest of your life you may want to look elsewhere for employment.

If so, did they enjoy the position?

If your employer answers "yes." Find out whether or not they enjoyed the position that you are going to fill. It is always beneficial to hear from someone who has already filled the shoes you are walking into.

Would they recommend that you take other steps before coming directly to the company?

Unbelievably, employers are more than willing to advise you to go a different direction during an interview. Most people are looking out for your best interest. So go ahead and ask them this question. The answer may be that you are exactly where you should be, or you may find that there is a better way to go about things. You will never know unless you ask.

These questions and more will help you evaluate the position in your own mind.

Does the employer feel that your qualities will help the organization grow?

This is the employer's chance to be honest with you, and let you know what he or she truly thinks about your traits. There is a chance he or she will let you know immediately that this is not the position for you. Although this may hurt at the time, at least the decision has been made for you, and you are able to move forward and look elsewhere.

What would be the one piece of advice you think I should take away from this interview?

Here is a fun question to ask. Even if the interview is not going well up to this point, you can still bring something away from the interview process. Your time is important, after all. This way you are always learning. If this is not the job for you, now you know what to look for in the future. The advice might be something you will hang on to for life. It is never a bad idea to gain advice from someone other than your immediate friends and family. It may help you nail the next interview.

Why do you enjoy working for this company?

This is an important question because this gives you some insight into what benefits the company gives without directly asking, "What benefits will I receive when working for this company?" When asked this question someone may list off things such as time off, vacation days, great health benefits, retirement plans, a friendly environment, and so on. All these things are important when looking into a specific position. You want to make sure that the company has attributes that you feel are necessary to survive in your daily work environment.

12

Communication

Communication plays a vital role in the workplace today. Effective communication, regardless of the style, requires two important skills. The most important is listening. Here is an excerpt from Podmoroff's book explaining the importance of communication:

"We hear so much today about the importance of communication or the ability to communicate with others, both in written and verbal formats. The difficulty in assessing or evaluating communication is that it necessarily involves two people. Effective communication for one person may be deemed ineffective by the other for no other reason than a difference in style. Does that make one of the parties a better or worse communicator? Not necessarily: it depends on the context. For a person employed in a job that involves public speaking, his or her communication style must have broad appeal in order to be considered effective. For the research scientist working in the lab, effective communication will likely involve much less flamboyance, but a direct and to-the-point style is not necessarily ineffective. Effective communication is about sending and receiving messages, so it is important not to have an idea set in stone about what constitutes effective communication before evaluating the purpose of the communication required."

This statement shows that there is not one particular form of communication that covers all bounds. It reinstates that we need to do our research before approaching an interview. Ask yourself, "What position am I interviewing for?" Depending on your answer, you need to do research in this particular field. Does the position require public speaking? If so, you want to project yourself in the interview. Show the employer that you have the ability to effectively communicate to crowds.

If the position you are interviewing for is in a line of work that requires interpersonal communication skills (one on one communicating or one on a few), do your best to illustrate your ability to effectively speak to a smaller group during the interview. The employer wants to see that you are a good fit for the position, and your ability to communicate plays a huge role in whether or not you are hired.

Everyone has different styles of to get their point across. As Podmoroff said, "Effective communication for one person may be deemed ineffective by the other for no other reason than a difference in style." Try to read the employer's body language. If, during the interview, you feel as if your style of communication is not working, please switch it up. Your goal here is to impress the employer. Prove to the interviewer that you have the ability to toggle your communication styles to fit others needs.

Being able to hear the message being sent is equally important to effective communication as being able to send a message. The second part of effective communication is, then, active listening. Listening for clues to discover the intent behind the message is vital for deciding how to respond and, thus, completing the communication cycle. An interview is an excellent forum to evaluate both sides of the communication equation; it involves active listening and clear expression. The interviewer should know by the end of the interview whether you are an effective communicator.

Without listening, there would be no communication. During the interview process, it is essential that you listen to the questions being asked of you. Efficient listening helps you see what the interviewer is looking for. Hearing what the interviewer is asking helps you give the interviewer the correct answers. You want to be sure to answer all questions in full. Employers tend to ask questions within questions. It will impress the employer if you are able to answer each aspect of the question without the employers repeating themselves. Show them you are listening.

Here is Joseph McCormack's answer to the question, "During a job interview, what are the key qualifications you are looking for?" "Obviously, the experience, skills, and education necessary to do the job. But beyond those givens, intelligence, energy, the ability to listen, and good communications skills. Brevity and focus are also important."

Listening

For good communication to occur, the message recipient must listen attentively to the speaker and provide the speaker with clues that he or she is being listened to. A simple nod of the head or affirmative response conveys to the speaker that their message is being heard and respected.

Listening is the most important part of the communicating process. During an interview, you want to show your interest in the interviewer's questions and comments. This can be done with simple gestures. As Podmoroff mentioned, the slight head nod conveys attentiveness. Regardless of the topic of conversation, keep your eyes on the interviewer. You want to maintain interest in the speaker and show that you are an effective communicator. This keeps you engaged in the conversation, and eliminates any embarrassing situations that might have occurred if you had not been listening.

While going over the case studies, I happened upon a question that it seems people enjoyed answering. When I asked, "Does your job influence the lives of other people?," I received many inspiring answers.

Craig Fowler: "My job as a corporate trainer most influences the lives of others. I would not be as happy doing it, if it did not. In addition, the roles that I train others to do most influence others as well. Recruiters affect the lives of everyone they touch. A recruiter has to be an excellent listener, salesperson, and, most importantly, honest. We are dealing with people's careers; it is not exactly life and death, but a person's livelihood is hugely important."

Joseph McCormack: "Yes, I am acutely aware that it does. Moving a candidate across country or persuading him or her to give up a secure position for a new opportunity both imply a moral responsibility. We are advocates for the employers who pay our fees, but we must also consider the fit, career goals, and happiness of the employee. It has to be a win-win situation."

Ken Sundheim: "Of course. As a recruiter, you directly influence the daily lives of others by finding them the right company and position. Work is an integral part of our lives, and it is my job to place people in the career that is going to make them happiest on a daily basis. Out of all the levels of applicants we deal with, I have the most impact on a recent college graduate's life. Following graduation, most people don't know what they want to do. Many times, their perceptions of corporate America are inaccurate. I make it a point to take the time to explain how careers differ, the future a particular career offers, what they should expect from their first job and other nuances which they are unaccustomed to, never having been in the working world, aside from an internship or two. As their careers progress, these people often call to seek my advice on their next move. This is very flattering, as it is evidence that I have made a difference in someone's life."

So choose a career in which you are able to answer "yes" as well. You do not have to necessarily go down in the history books but touching other people's lives is always beneficial. It seems as if these few executives have enjoyed their direct influence on the lives of others. Keep your eyes and ears peeled and listen to what people are telling you. Listening is a major key to all communication.

13

The Wrap Up

If you feel that the company is a match, when the interview is wrapping up, thank the interviewers for their time and efforts. You might say; "Thank you for you time. I have enjoyed meeting with you, and I am very interested in the opportunity. I feel that I am, with my education and background, a good match for the position. Can you tell me the next step in the interview process?"

Here is where you are showing your direct interest in the position and the company if you are interested. If you are attracted to and excited about the position, let it be known. An employer likes to hear that the interviewer was impressed, and will feed off your enthusiasm. Just as a house guest might say, "Thank you, we had a blast tonight," when leaving a party, show your interest. This gives the employer the opportunity to let you know exactly what is going to happen next. You do not want to leave the interview without knowing the next step in the process.

Next Step

Can you fill me in on what the next step is in the interviewing process?

Without asking a similar question, you are leaving the interview in the dark.

You want to make sure that you feel confident in what is going to happen next after the interview. People tend to get anxious about time. Do not hesitate to inquire about when you will hear their decision. If this is just the initial interview, and you know there is going to be a series of interviews to follow, ask when and where the next interview will be held.

In addition, as with whom the interview is going to be with?

Do not leave without a name. People tend to enjoy being called by their name. Find out a contact person in case there is a scheduling conflict is also necessary. Having a direct contact helps you if you need further insight down the road. A name and a phone number are necessary. It is always beneficial to get a card with e-mail as well.

Success

During my case studies the question was asked; "What brought you to the position you hold today?" Here are a few of the many great answers I received.

Craig Fowler: "A former colleague of mine (actually a former trainee of mine) called me one day and asked if I would like to be a full-time recruitment trainer. His company was looking to create a position for someone who would be responsible for training the current recruiters as well as any new employees. He called at the right time, as I was burning out of the position I was in previously. The timing and position were an answer to my prayer.

Joseph McCormack replied, "I entered the search business in 1976, after five years as a staff member for the Young Presidents' Organization, with the intention of starting my own practice. I spent my first five years learning the business from large search firms in New York and

Los Angeles, and launched my first venture with Jerry Farrow in 1982. McCormack & Farrow is now the largest retained search practice based in Orange County, California. I sold my interest in that firm to found McCormack & Associates in Los Angeles in 1993."

Ken Sundeim of KAS Placement describes what makes him successful in his line of business: "I strive to become the best I can be. I ensure that all my clients are taken care of and, no matter how particular their requests are, I deliver. I am able to see the candidates whom I place as people rather than sales machines. Only when someone sees that you can be trusted and are easy to work with can you form a strong bond with them. I am constantly trying to get better and I never stop learning. Through constant reading and listening, I become familiarized with different areas of expertise and fully expand my intellectual horizons. This knowledge affords me the ability to engage in meaningful conversations and develop a connection with almost any type of person. I also make sure to keep in shape. Dealing with people every day is unpredictable and, therefore stressful. Going for a run and/or lifting weights a few times a week makes a positive impact on how you feel and on your interaction with clients and candidates. I always want to be perceived as upbeat and put together; exercise helps me achieve these results."

Peter M. Sorensen illustrates his success: "Winning more often than loosing. Getting up after you have been knocked down. Surrounding yourself with good people."

Michael Maffei describes his success in the following way: "Though I have held many positions with multiple companies throughout my career, I stayed with one industry. That made it easier to move "up the ladder" and not appear like I didn't know what I wanted to do. This in turn allowed me to start my own company because I was seen as an expert in the call center industry and felt confident that I could succeed in my own business."

Craig Fowler: "Persistence is probably the most important quality. Able to tolerate ambiguity is up there on the list of what makes recruiters successful. Another quality that is extremely important is remaining a student of the field/industry. Healthcare is an ever-evolving industry, constantly in flux. So, remaining up-to-date with information makes recruiters relevant and credible; these are qualities that are invaluable in our field."

William Ronald describes his businesses success by stating, "We are successful in our line of business, because we offer a service that most teams need. The teams that visit our facility are high school and college programs. Unlike most companies, we do not see our business fluctuate with the economy. Schools dedicate money for sports programs, and most sports fundraise throughout the off-season for pre-season trips. We target teams from up north that participate in spring sports (baseball, softball, lacrosse, etc) because we know that before their season they cannot practice outside. They come to Florida to get out of the snow and start their season off to gain a competitive edge on other teams in their region.

We are also successful because of the opportunity we offer teams. They can eat, sleep, practice and play all in one location. A team never has to leave the complex if they do not want to. This also helps us because we are able to package the entire trip for the teams. Additionally, the facility is located 15 miles from the ocean, some of the teams have never seen the beach before, and this is their only chance."

Standards

Bob Clark sums up the question, "Is it possible to find the perfect job?" He states, "I believe it is possible to find the perfect job. Keep in mind however, that what might be the perfect job for you now, might not be the perfect job for you in the future. Consider a variety of criteria when deciding if the job is the perfect fit. Do you like the location? Is the compensation appropriate? Do you like the company's culture? Is the job in the area of practice/specialty/industry that you are interested in? All of these things are important in determining if you have, in fact, found the perfect job."

So make sure that the answers you have received during the interview process fit your standards. As stated above, if all of your standards have not been met, you have not found the perfect job. Finding the perfect job is the reason that you are in this situation in the first place. Keep in mind all of your preparation and compare what you have heard to your values, and principles. This decision is going to affect you and your loved ones directly, so do not take this situation lightly.

Thank You

Upon wrapping up the interview, if you feel as if this is not the position for you, it is still your responsibility to thank the interviewer for their time and efforts. You never know what your future is going to hold, and you want to be certain you leave a positive taste in the interviewer's mouths. This may help you inquire about a future opening or position with the company at a later date.

Regardless of how you felt the interview went, a heartfelt thank you is expected. Let the interviewers know that you appreciate the time they have given you to evaluate their company. Now that the interview is over with it is your time to depart. You have made it, Congratulations! All that is left to do is wait on a decision. Sometimes the waiting is the hardest part. Do not let the time get to you. Remember to follow up with the employer a day or two after the interview. Check in with them and thank them again.

One follow-up call or e-mail is sufficient. Be patient while waiting on an answer. The process takes time. Try to keep yourself from dwelling about the position. Instead keep your options open and stay busy interviewing and learning from other new experiences. The answer will come before you know it. The rest is up to the employer.

14

Case Studies

Below are answers to twenty original questions regarding interviewing strategies. I sent the participants these questions and requested that they answer ten questions of their choice in full. When finished they sent me their completed questionnaires. The answers that the participants gave to these questions are open and honest, and may give you some strategic insights for your next interview.

Below are the candidates and their unrehearsed answers to the questions asked of them.

CASE STUDY: CRAIG FOWLER

Craig Fowler, Vice President of Training and Business Development

Pinnacle Health Group

Personal Background . . .

Craig Fowler was born in Houston, Texas. He currently lives with his wife and two children, ages five and eight, with one on the way, in Stockbridge, Georgia (a suburb of Atlanta).

Professional Background. . .

Fowler has healthcare industry experience in clinical patient care and physician/corporate recruiting. This experience spans over 14 years with nearly ten of those years focused solely on physician recruitment.

CASE STUDY: CRAIG FOWLER

After completing his BA in psychology, he entered the workforce on the clinical side of health care. This experience affords Fowler a unique understanding of the medical facility's perspective. He started his career working with mentally ill patients in both inpatient and outpatient settings. He performed such tasks as maintaining patients' medical compliance, conducting mental status exams, and writing treatment and discharge plans for patients.

Fowler then transitioned to recruiting with a prominent physician-recruiting firm where he became a Director of Recruiting within two years, while earning his MBA. As a full-time recruiter, Fowler has worked searches in small rural communities as well as large healthcare systems and academic institutions. He has worked searches ranging from primary care to searches for super-sub specialists.

In his career to date, Fowler has personally mentored 30 recruiters, and has assisted in training over 50 recruiters as a team leader and trainer. He has also evaluated nearly 300 practice opportunities. Currently, Fowler is responsible for the training and development of new hires as well as seasoned recruiters at Pinnacle Health Group where he manages a team of recruiters and is intimately involved in the day-to-day activities of their searches. He also trains hospital staff on the basics of physician recruiting.

Additionally, Fowler holds the position of chair, School of Healthcare Recruitment for the National Association of Physician Recruiters. The 'school' offers the new and the experienced recruiter courses on topics relevant to in-house and fee-for-service recruiters. Fowler has also been asked to speak at residency programs on the topic "Helping Physicians Prepare for the Workforce." Most recently, he has trained on the topic "Keys to Effective Physician Recruitment" for the Medical Group Management Association (MGMA). This one-and-a-half-day course is part of the MGMA's "Core Learning Series."

As an author of articles on physician compensation, trainer of new and seasoned physician recruiters, and a speaker/trainer for such associations as the NAPR and the MGMA, Fowler is a recognized expert in the physician recruitment arena.

What brought you to the position you hold today?

A former colleague of mine (actually a former trainee of mine) called me one day and asked if I would like to be a full-time recruitment trainer. His company was looking to create a position for someone who would be responsible for training

CASE STUDY: CRAIG FOWLER

the current recruiters as well as any new employees. He called at the right time, as I was burning out of the position I was in previously. The timing and position were an answer to my prayer.

What do you feel is the most important question in a job interview?

"What is motivating you to make a change at this time?" This question will give the interviewer many directions to take the interview. It has the potential to give the interviewer a sense of the candidate's seriousness about making a change, it gives the interviewer insight as to how this person makes decisions, and it can give the interview a hint as to this person's attitude toward work.

Is it possible to find the perfect job?

No. Just like there are no perfect candidates. Last time I checked, there are no perfect people alive today; and, by definition, a "job" has workers and supervisors who are imperfect people.

Seriously, I tell candidates and clients, that if they have found 80 percent of what they are looking for in a job or a candidate, then they should strongly consider accepting the position or the candidate.

Who has influenced you the most in your career?

My family. I have been married for more than 12 years, and have two wonderful children (with one on the way). My wife is extremely supportive of my travels and late nights, and my kids are a joy. I live for them on the weekends. My wife is my biggest cheerleader and my fairest critic.

Does your job influence the lives of other people?

My job as a corporate trainer most definitely influences the lives of others. I would not be as happy doing it, if it did not. Also, the roles that I train others to do most definitely influence others as well. Recruiters affect the lives of everyone they touch. A recruiter has to be an excellent listener, salesperson, and, most importantly, honest. We are dealing with people's careers; it isn't exactly life and death, but a person's livelihood is hugely important.

During an interview what are the key qualifications you are looking for?

Natural confidence. In sales, which recruiting – at its core – is, everyone is confident. I am looking for an unrehearsed, natural, humble confidence. In addition, I am looking for someone who can speak well, someone who is

CASE STUDY: CRAIG FOWLER

articulate, someone who is friendly, and they have to be coach able. If the person has these qualities, then we can discuss their sales numbers, accomplishments, work ethic, etc.

What is the interviewing process like at your place of work?

We are a small recruiting and consulting firm, so our interview process is fairly simple, yet thorough. We start with a telephone interview with me, and then I send an electronic "work value" questionnaire. Once I score the questionnaire, I will schedule the candidate for a face-to-face interview with me. The second face to face is with our EVP (Ethics, Values, Professionalism) of recruiting and our CFO (Chief Financial Officer). The final face to face is with our CEO (Chief Executive Officer) and COO (Chief Operating Officer). All the parties then collectively decide if we should move forward.

Do you ask about someone's personal life during an interview?

It usually comes up from their end. I train recruiters about EEOC (Equal Employment Opportunity Commission) questioning, so I do not make a habit of "asking" about a candidate's personal life, as I want to avoid crossing any lines relative to marital status, age, religion, etc.

What makes you successful in your line of business?

Persistence is probably the most important quality. Able to tolerate ambiguity is up there on the list of what makes recruiters successful. Another quality that is extremely important is remaining a student of the field/industry. Healthcare is an ever-evolving industry, constantly in flux. So, remaining up-to-date with information makes recruiters relevant and credible; these are qualities that are invaluable in our field.

Can you tell if someone is prepared for an interview?

Absolutely! It shows in the questions that they ask me. If they are prepared, they have relevant questions to ask me. They have an understanding of our niche and how we approach the physician-recruiting marketplace

CASE STUDY: JOSEPH A. MCCORMACK

JOSEPH A. McCORMACK

Managing Partner

Joe McCormack is founder and managing partner of McCormack & Associates, Los Angeles. He has been a founding partner of the 23-year-old firm of McCormack & Farrow, the largest retained search practice in Orange County, California. As a partner in this practice, he was a founding Board Member of the International Association of Corporate Directors.

His 30 years of search experience include positions in New York and Los Angeles as partner with Ward Howell International, vice president with Ray & Berndtson and with Billington, Fox & Ellis, and manager with Ernst & Young.

He has served clients in nearly every sector of American business, filling senior-management and board positions in higher education, health care, and not-for-profit organizations. Clients have included Southern Methodist University, Washington State University, the University of California at Los Angeles, the American College of Physician Executives, the Los Angeles County Department of Public Health, PacifiCare, Fluor Corporation, Sea-Land Corporation, U.S. Borax, The Walt Disney Company, Hollywood Presbyterian Hospital, and Group Health Cooperative of Puget Sound.

Earlier, McCormack was a program director with the Young Presidents' Organization, an 8,000 member international educational association of corporate chief executives. As a staff executive with the Young Presidents' Organization in the 1970s, McCormack recruited corporate CEOs to the Boards of hospitals, colleges, and museums. He managed community relations and special events for Rockefeller Center in New York and promotion for American Heritage Publishing Co., Inc.

A graduate of the University of California at Berkeley, McCormack served in the U.S. Navy and, following training in the Department of Defense Information School, was a Naval public affairs officer on the staff of Commander, U.S. SECOND Fleet. He served for eight years as a director of Epilogics, Inc., a technology licensing company in northern California and four years on the national Board of the Gay, Lesbian, & Straight Education Network (GLSEN), which advocates for respect for all in our nation's schools. He presently serves on the Board of Regents for The Point Foundation, the first national LGBT scholarship fund. Previously, he served

CASE STUDY: JOSEPH A. MCCORMACK

as vice chairman of the Board of PHFE (Public Health Foundation Enterprises) in Los Angeles.

What brought me to the position I hold today, which is Managing Partner of McCormack & Associates, a retained executive search firm?

I entered the search business in 1976, after five years as a staff member for the Young Presidents' Organization, with the intention of starting my own practice. I spent my first five years learning the business from large search firms in New York and Los Angeles, and launched my first venture with Jerry Farrow in 1982. McCormack & Farrow is now the largest retained search practice based in Orange County, California. I sold my interest in that firm to found McCormack & Associates in Los Angeles in 1993.

How did you find your interviewing process?

I assume you mean, "How did I learn to interview?"

As a Manager with Arthur Young Executive Resource Consultants in the 1970s, I received formal training in every aspect of recruiting from research to reference checks. I have obviously also learned from the many skilled interviewers I've worked with over the years, taken refresher courses from time to time, and developed my own style and technique based on 30 years of practice.

What do you feel is the most important question in a job interview?

I assume you mean, "What is the most important question for a candidate to ask?"

After a candidate has exchanged pleasantries with the interviewer, I would ask, "Before we begin, please tell me what the most important things are that you need to know about my background or experience for this position so that I can be focused and helpful in my responses to your questions."

Have you ever witnessed a perfect interview?

Yes. The elements of a perfect interview are:

   a. Thorough preparation and research on the position and the organization

   b. A brief but strong opening statement of interest

   c. Brief but focused responses to questions with one or two examples to illustrate each point

CASE STUDY: JOSEPH A. MCCORMACK

   d.   Good questions about the position and organization based upon homework

   e.   A closing statement that sums up a candidate's qualifications

   f.   A sense of humor throughout the meeting

Does your job influence the lives of other people?

Yes, I am acutely aware that it does. Moving a candidate across country or persuading him or her to give up a secure position for a new opportunity both imply a moral responsibility. We are advocates for the employers who pay our fees, but we must also consider the fit, career goals, and happiness of the employee. It has to be a win-win situation.

During a job interview, what are the key qualifications you are looking for?

Obviously, the experience, skills, and education necessary to do the job. But beyond those givens, intelligence, energy, the ability to listen, and good communications skills. Brevity and focus are also important.

How long have you held your current position?

Fourteen years as Managing Partner of McCormack & Associates.

Do you ask about someone's personal life during an interview?

Within the bounds of legality, yes. I am interested in what motivated a candidate to choose his or her career, who has been a role model or influence, what they value in an employer, etc., Issues about health are only permissible within the context of ability to do a job, but questions about how a candidate handles stress, what he or she does to relax or recharge a depleted battery can lead to some interesting discussions. If travel is involved, we need to establish that this would not be a hardship for the candidate.

Does the pace of interview change if the candidate is noticeably nervous?

I do my very best to put a candidate at ease because I believe that a relaxed candidate will be more forthcoming and honest than one under stress. If I sense that a candidate is nervous, I tell personal stories or leaven the conversation with humor. It helps to break up the "hard" interview questions with a bit of conversation from time to time.

Can you tell if someone is prepared for an interview?

CASE STUDY: JOSEPH A. MCCORMACK

Yes. It's apparent from their knowledge of the hiring organization and/or the position and its responsibilities.

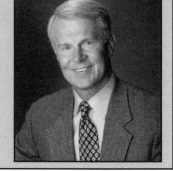

CASE STUDY: KEN SUNDHEIM

Ken Sundheim

KAS Placement, New York
305 East 86th St. #3FW
New York, NY 10028
www.kasplacement.com.

A little bit about myself and company:

My name is Ken Sundheim. I am president and owner of KAS Placement, a New York based recruiting firm. We serve clients in 15 countries spanning three different continents. Primarily, KAS Placement assists sales professionals in all different industries find new, challenging careers.

When needed, we also help our clients find accounting and finance professionals. On occasion we place high-end personal assistants for both celebrities and wealthy individuals. Over the years, we have successfully worked with companies in the following mediums: insurance, finance, real-estate, technology, compliance, textiles, translations, import/export, telecommunications, transportation, gaming, publishing, beauty and food.

Prior to opening KAS Placement, I worked as a sales representative for a small firm, which specialized in financial compliance software and Microsoft Exchange hosting. Following my experience in technology sales, I took a position as an account manager for a large, Minnesota-based financial services vendor. My key accounts were Chase, Washington Mutual and Bank of New York.

CASE STUDY: KEN SUNDHEIM

My love for sales eventually drove me to leave my job and open a recruiting firm. Like most businesses, we were started with little capital from a home-based office. Soon, I found myself too busy, got an office space and began to grow the company. As I hoped, KAS Placement rapidly became a very successful, lucrative placement agency with a very large and loyal client base.

What do you feel is the most important question in a job interview?

I have a firm belief that there is not one single question that is as important as having an upbeat personality, presentable dress, being on time, being knowledgeable about the subjects in which you're conversing and making a personal connection with the person on the other side of the table.

Nevertheless, in my opinion, the most significant interview question would be a variation of the following: "What are the main differentials of your product and your competitor's and how do you leverage those differences to win business?"

Have you ever witnessed a perfect interview?

This is a prudent, yet tricky question. Yes and no. I have come across dozens of very intelligent, personable people who can effectively answer nearly any question at the drop of a dime. In that sense, they are perfect.

However, a flawless interview is a matter of opinion. I have often been surprised at the some of my clients' (employers) assessments of a person and their interview skills. To give you an example, I was working with a company in Philadelphia who wanted to see five applicants in order to fill a vacant sales management slot. After narrowing the field down to five, I had subconsciously picked the person I thought to be the most qualified and the person whom I perceived to be the least qualified. Surprisingly my client chose the person who I thought was a back-runner. This just goes to show that interview perfection is merely a matter of opinion. Although I have been exceptionally impressed with some interviews, I would be hard pressed to describe any as entirely faultless.

Is it possible to find the perfect job?

It is my belief that work is part of something we do everyday to stay busy, generate income and feel fulfilled. It is possible to find the job that best suits your personality, work ethic and desired compensation, but to find a profession where every single task proves joyous is exceedingly hard. Like human beings, all jobs are bound to have small imperfections.

CASE STUDY: KEN SUNDHEIM

Who has influenced you the most in your career?

My wife, Alison - Ali also works at KAS Placement. She left her job in public relations and came to work with me about eight months after starting KAS Placement. She is someone in the business whom I can be honest with, bounce ideas off of and rely on to give 100percent of her efforts on every project. Most business owners do not have the luxury of getting an honest opinion from their co-workers or subordinates; if it wasn't for my wife, I would not have had the success I've enjoyed.

My mother and father – I speak to my father every day; he is my biggest fan. My mother is a great at listening without judgment and, throughout my life, has always been supportive of me.

Harvey Cohen - Harvey is my mentor and owns a very successful technology-recruiting firm by the name of Finders Agency. Harvey is my sister-in-law's father. When I was first starting out, Harvey would take as much time as necessary to assist me with any and all issues that came up. Although we have different styles, Harvey taught me the business. I do not think I could have accomplished what I have without his guidance, love and support.

What are your suggestions for someone who is trying to find a career in your line of work?

Similar to any field, you must be cautious of the type of employment agency you choose. Some recruiting firms are great and are full of intelligent, successful people. However, because there is a low entry bar and minimal base salary, many firms are not selective about their employee pool and are unpleasant places to work. They often see their success and financial resources quickly drained.

When entering the field, it is best to begin with a specialty and get very good at it. You have to think to yourself, "Do I want to be in law recruitment, sales recruitment, technology recruitment or some other facet?" You should go with what interests you. If you do not like computers, stay away from IT recruiting firms.

I would also suggest reading a book on recruiting. Being a headhunter is not for everyone. In most cases, there is no steady paycheck, as most firms provide health insurance and pay on commission; you must prepare yourself for that. Be aware that this business is very competitive and economically sensitive. When the times are good, they are great and when corporate hiring slows, it seems as

CASE STUDY: KEN SUNDHEIM

if the office is a ghost town. Get to know the lay of the land as well as the ups and downs before diving into recruitment.

Does your job influence the lives of other people?

Of course. As a recruiter, you directly influence the daily lives of others by finding them the right company and position. Work is an integral part of our lives, and it is my job to place people in the career that is going to make them happiest on a daily basis.

Out of all the levels of applicants we deal with, I have the most impact on a recent college graduate's life. Following graduation, most people do not know what they want to do. Many times, their perceptions of corporate America are inaccurate. I make it a point to take the time to explain how careers differ, the future a particular career offers, what they should expect from their first job and other nuances which they are unaccustomed to, never having been in the working world, aside from an internship or two. As their careers progress, these people often call to seek my advice on their next move. This is very flattering, as it is evidence that I have made a difference in someone's life.

During an interview what are the key qualifications you are looking for?

Simply put: intelligence, effective communication, a good education, ambition, sincerity, drive, relevant experience and past success.

What does it take to become a member of your current organization?

When I hire employees, I look for a few must-haves. If any of these traits or skills is not present, I pass. First, it is a must that everyone whom I work with (or works at my company) has very strong writing and verbal skills. In my line of work, you have to be able to effectively work with and gain the respect of many different types of people. In business, people only follow and respect those can quickly and consistently demonstrate their intelligence.

They must also have a friendly, caring personality. I began KAS Placement on the premise that we would be different from other companies. Instead of seeing an applicant as a quick buck, I make sure to care about the needs of the people with whom we work. The same is expected from everyone at my company. As a headhunter, if all you care about is the money an applicant will generate, it will be apparent to your candidates and sour your reputation.

CASE STUDY: KEN SUNDHEIM

I also need everybody in the office to be able to use his or her intelligence to its fullest extent. I want people who want to make a difference in my company. When I hire someone, I do not just hire him or her for his or her recruiting skills. I want someone who has a drive to make the company better. I want to see them act as if they owned KAS Placement themselves.

Do you ask about someone's personal life during an interview?

As an interviewer, I make it a point to stay away from personal questions unless they are common questions like where do you live, how was your Thanksgiving, etc. In human resources, you can get into a lot of trouble if you attempt to dig too deep into another's personal life.

What makes you successful in your line of business?

I strive to become the best I can be. I ensure that all my clients are taken care of and, no matter how particular their requests are, I deliver. I am able to see the candidates whom I place as people rather than sales machines. Only when someone sees that you can be trusted and are easy to work with can you form a strong bond with him or her.

I am constantly trying to get better and I never stop learning. Through constant reading and listening, I become familiarized with different areas of expertise and fully expand my intellectual horizons. This knowledge affords me the ability to engage in meaningful conversations and develop a connection with almost any type of person.

I also make sure to keep in shape. Dealing with people everyday is unpredictable and, therefore stressful. Going for a run and/or lifting weights a few times a week makes a positive impact on how you feel and on your interaction with clients and candidates. I always want to be perceived as upbeat and put together; exercise helps me achieve these results.

Can you tell if someone is prepared for an interview?

Instantly. You can read it in their body language and voice. People who are unprepared tend not to be as enthusiastic and often appear lackadaisical or nervous. Over time, the extent of interview preparation done by a particular applicant has become very easy to decipher. I can usually determine whether or not an applicant has prepared his or her thoughts prior to an interview and, subsequently, competent enough for further consideration within ten to thirty seconds of conversation.

CASE STUDY: MICHAEL R. MAFFEN

Michael R. Maffei
President & Managing Partner

The BrandonWayne Group is a dedicated team of call center professionals led by industry veteran Michael R. Maffei. Maffei has over 25 years of call center industry experience working with some of the world's leading companies. He is also a recognized industry speaker, seminar leader and consultant. Maffei is a certified Six-Sigma Black Belt and was part of an organization that won the prestigious Malcolm Baldridge Award.

Maffei has been a speaker at a variety of call center events across North America during the past two decades. He is frequently noted in trade journals and has been interviewed or quoted in call center industry publications such as Call Center Magazine and Customer Interface Magazine.

During the course of his career, Mr. Maffei was vice president for a major staffing company where he built an organization that generated almost $80 million in call center staffing business in three years. He was a principal consultant for PricewaterhouseCoopers, where he led call center consultative engagements for Fortune 100 companies. As a Senior Director for an outsourcing company, Mr. Maffei led engagements worldwide for new call center program implementations. He has directly managed multiple site call centers and started his career on the phones.

Though experienced in all phases and areas of call center operations, Mr. Maffei's real passion and expertise is helping call centers solve their number one issue and cost component; the recruiting, hiring and retention of call center personnel.

Mr. Maffei has a Bachelor's Degree in Business Administration from the Eugene W. Stetson School of Business and Economics at Mercer University in Macon, Georgia.

What brought you to the position you hold today?

I started my company in 2003 because I saw a need in the marketplace for a company that specialized in call center recruiting and staffing at all levels. I personally have over 25 years of experience in the call center industry.

What do you feel is the most important question in a job interview?

CASE STUDY: MICHAEL R. MAFFEN

That's easy and it's a question that I use in every interview, regardless of the type or level of the position. "Why are you here today?" That one simple question tells me a lot about the individual.

Have you ever witnessed a perfect interview?

There is no such thing. Having done this for so many years, I can tell fairly easily who is rehearsed and who is natural. My job is to read between the lines during an interview. It's OK to be prepared and confident, just be yourself. Not every job is going to be a "perfect fit"; no matter how qualified you may "think" you are.

Where do you suggest someone go when looking for a career?

Networking is still the best way. Your friends, family, former business associates, college alumni associations and career and trade groups are great sources. Let everyone know you are actively looking. There is no reason not to explore all those options. With the employment environment the way it is, everyone has looked for a job, probably multiple jobs, so utilize the people and resources you know best. They will want to help because they have probably been helped by someone themselves in their job search.

My advice to job seekers has always been to treat the job search as if it were your job; especially if you are unemployed. Spend eight-to-ten hours a day in your search and you'll be surprised at the results.

Is it possible to find the perfect job?

There is an old saying, Love what you do and then you'll have the perfect job. Once you lose that feeling, then it just becomes another job.

What are your suggestions for someone who is trying to find a career in your line of work?

The great thing about the call center industry is that there will always be a need for qualified people. Over 3 percent of the US workforce is employed in some type of call center type position. There are over 50,000 call centers in the United States. Though entry level positions can be lower wages with odd hours, management positions pay well and they longer you stay, the more opportunity you will have. Bottom line, if you have at least five or more years of call center management experience, good paying jobs are plentiful.

Do you ask about someone's personal life during an interview?

CASE STUDY: MICHAEL R. MAFFEN

Absolutely, part of the interview process is getting to know the person personally. There not only has to be a skill fit for the position, but also a cultural fit for the organization. Because of EEOC guidelines, you have to be very careful about questions of this nature, but it is perfectly reasonable to have a conversation about a candidate's time outside of work. This tends to relax the candidate more during the interview process, and what person doesn't love talking about things they enjoy like family, sports, etc.

Does the pace of the interview change is the person is noticeably nervous?

Almost everyone has butterflies before an interview. If you don't, you're not human. I always looked at interviews as a challenge. Though I may have been nervous, I stayed focus on the interviewer's body language and line of questioning. That will tell you a lot about the pace of the interview. You have to be able to adjust to the style of your interviewer. They certainly will not adjust to you.

A lot of times, the interviewer is also nervous. My job is to insure the candidate is relaxed and comfortable. A lot of interviews fail, not because of the person being interviewed, but because the interviewer was bad, they were rushed, or the environment the interview was taking place in was not the best. It's a two way street. Unfortunately, there are a lot of people doing interviews that shouldn't be.

What makes you successful in your line of business?

Though I have held many positions with multiple companies throughout my career, I stayed with one industry. That made it easier to move "up the ladder" and not appear like I didn't know what I wanted to do. This in turn allowed me to start my own company because I was seen as an expert in the call center industry and felt confident that I could succeed in my own business.

Can you tell if someone is prepared for an interview?

In the first minute, I can tell whether the interview is going to be successful or not. Remember, the first question I ask is "Why are you here today?" If they can't answer that with confidence, then the interview will typically not go very well.

CASE STUDY: KRISTIE WEHE

Kristie Wehe

Westaff

What brought you to the position you hold today?

Careful thought about my skills, previous positions I'd held, and what I felt would ultimately suit me. I asked myself about things like what I wanted from my career, what I needed in terms of money, etc.

What are your suggestions for someone who is trying to find a career in your line of work?

Persistence is imperative. Ask a lot of questions (like the ones in this book) during the interviewing process to make sure you are finding the right fit for you. Make phone calls, do not rely on e-mail. If it's important to you, pick up the phone, and let them know it's important.

How does your company compare to its competitors?

I think this is a great question, because if they can't tell you this right off the bat, something is wrong. And it's important to know if the interviewer at least believes that the company has a terrific reputation in the marketplace, if they are going to grow and continue to hire, etc. I chose Westaff because of their reputation, and the professionalism of the recruiter. And because, even though they weren't the biggest or the most well-known, they had a strong presence in the marketplace, and a solid reputation with both their candidates and their clients.

What is the interviewing process like at your place of work?

The whole team interviews every prospective candidate, and I think it's relatively intense because we do this for a living. We ask a lot of situational questions, and we're looking for honest answers, not necessarily the most polished.

How long have you held your current position?

A little more than two years.

What does it take to become a member of your current organization?

Depends on what position you are looking for. Generally speaking, we are looking for professional people with a passion for the industry.

CASE STUDY: KRISTIE WEHE

Do you ask about someone's personal life during an interview?

Generally no, but it does depend on what position they are interviewing for, and the kinds of responses they give. Sometimes they lead you to ask questions. Usually if someone is moving into the area, I will ask him or her why.

What makes you successful in your line of business?

Persistence. Organization. Follow-through. Passion.

What makes your company's interview process unique?

I think the fact that every team member is involved in the interview for internal hires. We are a small team, so it is important that everyone be sold on the new person.

Can you tell if someone is prepared for an interview?

Absolutely. By how they present themselves, by the questions they ask, by the interest and thoroughness they show in answering my questions. How they are dressed is a clue.

CASE STUDY: WILLIAM RONALD

William Ronald

Assistant Athletic Director Cocoa Expo Sports Center

Where do you suggest someone go when looking for a career?

Nowadays the internet is probably the best source for an employee looking for a career. Most industries have specific Web sites that list only jobs in the field that the employee is looking for. They can search using specific criteria. Most of these are pay services, but it is worth it because employers are more likely to post there jobs there.

Who has influenced you the most in your career?

The young general managers of professional sports teams have influenced me the most.

CASE STUDY: WILLIAM RONALD

What are your suggestions for someone who is trying to find a career in your line of work?

Complete at least one major internship to get your foot in the door. There are many positions out there, but the community is very small. It will not be too difficult to make a good name for yourself as a pro-active hard worker. On the other hand you can also make a bad name for yourself easily.

During an interview what are the key qualifications you are looking for?

Good communication skills, good personality, passion for sports, past experience running events, experience dealing one-on-one with people in pressure situations.

How does your company compare to its competitors?

We do not compare to our competitors in many ways. We are the only privately owned multi-sport complex with the ability to house and feed players in the same location. Other companies do the same thing that we do, but they use county- or city-owned fields and parks. In addition, other companies are not able to house and feed the players at the facility; this means teams are either one, required to find housing on their own, or two, find meals on their own or both, and the company will only setup the games/ practices.

Some of our competitors require players to purchase a certain number of park tickets as well, so on top of the entire fee is associated with the baseball training, teams must purchase park passes for one or more days.

What is the interviewing process like at your place of work?

Potential employees are interviewed via a brief telephone interview, and then are asked to come to the office for a formal interview with our general manager and athletics director at the same time. The interview takes anywhere from 20 – 45 minutes. The field is then narrowed and a candidate is chosen for the position. Two formal interviews may be necessary to make a decision.

How long have you held your current position?

One Year.

What does it take to become a member of your current organization?

Must possess a knowledge of sports, this includes the rules, regulations and play of particular sports. You must be able to plan organize and direct events. Marketing of events is a daily task.

CASE STUDY: WILLIAM RONALD

Does the pace of the interview change is the person is noticeably nervous?

There is a difference between noticeably nervous and uncomfortably nervous. A person should be nervous at a job interview, to me it shows that they are excited about the position and company, and really want the job. If they didn't they wouldn't be nervous. Noticeably nervous does not change the pace of the interview, uncomfortably nervous does.

What makes you successful in your line of business?

We are successful in our line of business, because we offer a service that most teams need. The teams that visit our facility are high school and college programs. Unlike most companies, we do not see our business fluctuate with the economy. Schools dedicate money for sports programs, and most sports fundraise throughout the off-season for pre-season trips. We target teams from up north that participate in spring sports (baseball, softball, lacrosse, etc) because we know that before their season they cannot practice outside. They come to Florida to get out of the snow and start their season off to gain a competitive edge on other teams in their region.

We are also successful because of the opportunity we offer teams. They can eat, sleep, practice and play all in one location. A team never has to leave the complex if they do not want to. This also helps us because we are able to package the entire trip for the teams. Additionally, the facility is located 15 miles from the Ocean, some of the teams have never seen the beach before, and this is their only chance.

How many positions have you had throughout you career?

One summer internship, two full-time positions (one year each).

Can you tell if someone is prepared for an interview?

I think if someone is not prepared for an interview their questions are textbook answers and it seems as if they are reading from queue cards. It is hard to be completely prepared for any interview because interviewers can be so different. But it is essential for a potential employee to research the company and be able to speak intelligently about it.

CASE STUDY: WESTLY KUSER

Westly Kuser

What do you feel is the most important question in a job interview?

Describe a scenario when you performed well under pressure.

Where do you suggest someone go when looking for a career?

College career fairs are a great place for entry-level employees to network and see professionals in all different types of careers.

Is it possible to find the perfect job?

I think it is possible to find the perfect job, when you are paid to do something that you enjoy doing and are passionate about, it isn't considered work.

Who has influenced you the most in your career?

My general manager at a College Baseball League- he showed me how to be successful in a career in sports. He also taught me the importance that a sports team has in a small town.

What are your suggestions for someone who is trying to find a career in your line of work?

Find an internship with a sports franchise/ facility that you would like to work for one day. Many companies hire within, as an intern, you will stand out to a GM or president if you do a good job and will have a great chance to turn that internship into a full-time position.

During an interview what are the key qualifications you are looking for?

Prior experience and willingness to learn are the most important qualifications in my line of work. I also look for employees that are open-minded and work well in teams. I need someone on my staff that has a good business sense.

Do you ask about someone's personal life during an interview?

Yes and no, I want to find out about their personal experiences pertaining to a working environment. I would not ask questions that are too personal.

Does the pace of the interview change is the person is noticeably nervous?

CASE STUDY: WESTLY KUSER

Yes, it is not hard to tell when someone is nervous. When an interviewee is comfortable, they are able to think clearer about their answers, therefore it is easier to tell what kind of person they really are.

What makes you successful in your line of business?

My attitude and openness to new ideas have been the key to my success.

Can you tell if someone is prepared for an interview?

When a person is not prepared for their interview their answers come off as scripted, they seem to be telling you what they think you want to hear, rather then what they think. It is easy to tell when this is happening.

CASE STUDY: PETER M. SORENSEN

Peter M. Sorensen
President
Dane Contracting, Inc.
P.O. Box 033663
Indialantic, FL 32903
State Certified General Contractors
danecontracting@cfl.rr.com

What brought you to the position you hold today?

Help from family, friends, and business relationships. Education and continuing education as well. Years of experience.

Is it possible to find the perfect job?

Yes, but it is rare in today's business place. Like in life, a good attitude toward your job can bring you happiness and wellbeing.

What are your suggestions for someone who is trying to find a career in your line of work?

Shotgun pattern your approach. Apply for jobs in multiple locations. Try to think of businesses/positions that might offer similar situations to your dream job. Check with trade organizations the companies you are interested in might belong to.

Does your job influence the lives of other people?

Yes, the customer satisfied will contact us again. The employee that does a

CASE STUDY: PETER M. SORENSEN

good job is needed on a continuing basis. The suppliers we use are rewarded by our patronage.

How does your company compare to its competitors?

We are customer geared. We try to give the customer what they. That is usually a quick response to their project, quick performance and professional craftsmen.

We try to give better, friendlier, low-cost service to our customers, so they will give us repeat business. We have longer track records with our customers and a broader customer base than most of our competitors.

What makes you successful in your line of business?

Winning more often than losing. Getting up after you've been knocked down. Surrounding yourself with good people.

How many positions have you had throughout you career?

About a dozen, ranging from high-school jobs to business ownership.

Can you tell if someone is prepared for an interview?

Yes, it is very obvious.

CASE STUDY: BILL PUCKETT

Bill Puckett
Managing Partner
Searchline Services, Inc.
1440 Rockside Road Ste 103
Cleveland, Oh. 44134
Phone 216 749 2820

I always like to ask the Candidate to tell me about a time in his or her life when they thought they were going to be killed.

The purpose of this question is that Candidates do a lot of acting and trying to be someone they think you are looking for and not be themselves. When they start telling a story about how they almost lost their lives, they get so emotionally involved in the story that they forget to act the part they are acting and they become more themselves. I have seen Candidates have completely different accents when they are telling me their life threatening story.

CASE STUDY: BOB CLARKE

Bob Clarke

Chief Executive Officer

Furst Group

Bob Clarke, Co-founder and CEO of Furst Group, has more than 20 years of executive search experience. In 1984, Bob joined a regional executive search firm (The Furst Group), where he developed a national division focused on health care executive recruitment. He led the acquisition in 1991 of this specialized practice, now known simply as Furst Group.

At Furst Group, Bob has been responsible for recruiting more than 300 senior executives for top positions with hospital systems, health maintenance organizations, preferred provider organizations, medical groups, indemnity companies, end-of-life providers, health care associations, and other medical delivery systems across the United States. Bob's work includes consulting with boards of directors of health care organizations to determine organizational readiness, manage senior staff transitions, develop succession plans, assess leadership teams, and implement leadership development programs. He has been responsible for building high-performance, high-growth teams at numerous organizations.

Bob is a frequent speaker on issues regarding effective leadership design, team selection and development, managed care and provider relationships, and the role of key leadership. He has led workshops and conducted presentations through organizations such as the Health Care Financial Management Association (HFMA), the America's Health Insurance Plans (AHIP), the Academy of Managed Care Pharmacy (AMCP), the National Hospice and Palliative Care Organization (NHPCO), and Florida Hospices and Palliative Care, Inc., as well as various physician executive MBA programs.

He has authored studies on executive leadership issues for a variety of health care fields and regularly serves as an expert resource for health care publications. As one of the top 10 executive recruiters in health care according to "The New Career Makers," Bob has been quoted in books and publications on the issues of leadership for the health care industry.

Currently on the Board of the Foundation for Hospices in Sub-Saharan African,

CASE STUDY: BOB CLARKE

which is part of the National Hospice and Palliative Care Organization (NHPCO), Bob has served on numerous boards and committees for organizations such as the American Association of Health Plans (renamed America's Health Insurance Plans) and the NHPCO Ethics Committee. He also was recently involved with NHPCO's Executive Leadership Program, which assists in the leadership training and course offerings for hospice leaders. In addition, he is a past member of the Board of Directors for the Northern Illinois Hospice and Grief Center, Visiting Nurses Association and for the American Red Cross, Rock River Chapter. Bob holds a Bachelor of Science degree in Business Administration and a Certified Managed Care Executive certificate.

About Furst Group

Furst Group, the seventh largest retained executive search firm in the health care industry, provides a "total solution" approach to traditional executive search, as well as an array of consulting products known as Human Capital Integration. Clients include managed care organizations, hospitals and health systems, integrated delivery systems, medical group practices, ancillary companies, insurance companies and end-of-life care businesses. Founded in 1984, Furst Group is headquartered in Rockford, Illinois, and has offices in Minneapolis, Washington D.C., Phoenix, Dallas and Seattle.

For more information, visit **www.furstgroup.com.**

Furst Group Interview questions

Bob Clark, CEO, Furst Group

What do you feel is the most important question in a job interview?

The most important question asked in a job interview is: 'Why do you want this job?" It sets the direction for the rest of the interview. If the answer focuses primarily on the money, title or location, the interview will be short in length. If the response deals with interests, motivation and values of the candidate, it will strike a more positive note and set the right tone for what is to follow.

Have you ever witnessed a perfect interview?

I don't believe there is such a thing. While I have often finished an interview thinking, 'that went really well', typically there is a question I forgot to ask or a topic I should have delved into further. I do think it is good advice for candidates and interviewers to make sure that those forgotten questions don't get dropped.

CASE STUDY: BOB CLARKE

From the candidate's perspective it is a good way to follow up after the interview.

Where do you suggest someone go when looking for a career? Talk to people you know, like and respect. Find out what they do and it might give you some ideas about what career path you might consider. Get to know people in areas you are interested in and network – it could lead to possible referrals and career opportunities.

Is it possible to find the perfect job?

I believe it is possible to find the perfect job. Keep in mind however, that what might be the perfect job for you now, might not be the perfect job for you in the future. Consider a variety of criteria when deciding if the job is the perfect fit. Do you like the location? Is the compensation appropriate? Do you like the company's culture? Is the job in the area of practice/specialty/industry that you are interested in? All of these things are important in determining if you have, in fact, found the perfect job.

During an interview what are the key qualifications you are looking for?

In addition to making sure that the candidate has the technical skills required for the position, I really try to delve into the candidate's interests, motivation and values. This is so important to determine a candidate as the 'right fit' for the position.

Do you ask about someone's personal life during an interview?

While you can not ask specific personal questions about religious affiliation, ethnicity, or marital status, a discussion about the candidate's personal life often comes up in the course of the conversation. If the candidate offers the information it is sometimes helpful in discovering more about his/her personality and if they would be a good fit for the organization.

Does the pace of the interview change if the person is noticeably nervous?

It can, and that's why it's important for the interviewer to put the interviewee at ease. It's helpful to talk about non-work related topics first in order to make the interview more conversational and informal. Creating an environment that allows the interviewee to open up is crucial in conducting a successful interview.

What makes your company's interview process unique?

CASE STUDY: BOB CLARKE

As a retained search firm we work with our clients to find the best possible candidate to fit their needs. Therefore, it's very important that we understand our clients' culture, mission and vision.

As the link between client and candidate, we must be as transparent and candid as possible. Emotions can, and do run high throughout the process and by providing as much information as possible puts our clients and the candidates at ease.

Can you tell if someone is prepared for an interview?

Yes, I think it is pretty obvious when candidates come prepared for the interview. They have good questions, have previewed the profile material and refer to it in their responses to questions. From the interviewer's perspective it is a lot easier interview when the candidate is prepared because there is a good exchange of information and the flow of the interview is dynamic. It is also very obvious when someone is not prepared for the interview. I am always looking for those candidates who come prepared because to me that is a clear indication of interest. If not, you have to wonder if they are really interested in the position.

Does your job influence the lives of other people?

Most definitely. The work we do influences the lives of other people, because we are working to find the best candidates for jobs in the health care field. The executives we place manage major hospitals and health systems, managed care plans, medical groups, hospice organizations, specialty service, and insurance companies. They are at the forefront of medical care, and their decisions affect millions. So of course the work we do is taken with the utmost care and responsibility.

Our work also influences the lives of the candidate and their families as they often face relocation and a new career direction.

Glossary

Below are some definitions that Podmoroff has described that may help you during the interviewing process.

Competency Definition: Accountability takes personal responsibility for outcomes.

Adapting to Change: Is very flexible and adaptable; copes well with change.

Business Mindedness: Understands the nature of the company's business and how his or her own role affects the bottom line.

Communication: Expresses oneself well verbally.

Conflict Management: Finds common ground to resolve issues.

Cooperation and Collaboration: Works well with others to achieve business and team goals.

Creating: Makes vision real to everyone

Communicating: One's vision inspiring another's vision.

Critical Thinking: Develops solutions to business problems.

Customer Focus: Concentrates on customers' best interests.

Dealing with Ambiguity: Embraces change and can comfortably handle risk and uncertainty.

Detail-Oriented: Is meticulous and precise in approach; quality-conscious and thorough.

Development: Improves oneself or others professionally.

Drive for Results: Consistently meets/exceeds goals; is action-oriented and passionate about the work; seizes opportunities.

Functional Knowledge: Well-developed knowledge of own functional area of expertise.

Influencing Others: Negotiates "win-win" outcomes in tough situations.

Initiative: Demonstrates self-motivation through action.

Innovation: Generates creative new ideas.

Integrity/Ethical: Behavior is trustworthy and demonstrates strong personal and professional values.

Interpersonal Skills: Relates well to all kinds of people at all levels within and outside the organization.

Leadership Potential: Motivates and inspires others.

Learning: Attitude pursues learning with drive and vigor.

Maintaining: Is tolerant of people and composure/flexibility processes and can deal well with change and new information.

Management Skills: Sets employee goals; coaches and monitors performance.

Managerial Courage: Does not hold back; makes tough decisions even when those decisions are unpopular.

Motivating Others: Empowers others to succeed.

Planning and Organizing Uses time and resources efficiently to accomplish work objectives.

Priority and Goal Setting: Quickly discovers the source of problems and generates thoughtful, effective solutions.

Problem Solving: Takes control of challenging projects with foresight and implementation focus.

Project Planning: Focuses effort on most important goals and objectives.

Risk Taking: Takes well-calculated business risks, learning from mistakes and false starts.

Service Orientation: Committed to meeting and exceeding customer expectations.

Strategic Agility: Is visionary; anticipates future consequences and trends.

Teamwork: Works well with others to achieve shared goals.

Technical Knowledge: Accurately and consistently and proficiently applies technical principles and practice to situations on the job.

Time Management: Uses time effectively and efficiently, concentrating efforts on most important priorities.

Works Independently: High degree of comfort operating autonomously.

Author Biography

When given the challenge to write this book I was thoroughly excited. I have found myself in the interview chair on a variety of occasions. People say that they grew up and always knew what they wanted to be. I on the other hand had a different approach. I always knew what I wanted to do in the moment, but never for the long run. Therefore, I have found myself as the interviewee many times. That said I consider myself a sort of connoisseur at interviews.

I have been fortunate enough to have been offered a variety of positions. I guess you can say that I am charming in the interview room. Even though I have been offered many positions and accepted most of them, I still do not know what I want to "be" when I grow up. I am constantly changing, and I always want something different, something more. My husband says that as long as I do not change him then we are all OK. Therefore, I am planning to continue to change and pursue new tasks. Although sometimes stressful, I find it fun and challenging.

I enjoy the challenge of taking on something new. I find it amazing that people can be whatever they want to be. You just have to jump through the necessary hoops to get there. Anyone can do anything. That is what I have learned throughout my experiences. As I have gone through many interviews, I have so much to say and even more insight on how the process works.

Each company obviously has their own way of going about things, whether it is an entire team interviewing you or just one person. From personality assessments to "good cop, bad cop" scenarios, I have seen it all. Incredibly, I live to tell the stories. Better yet, I have learned so much from each experience, and I am prepared to share this beneficial information with you.

Be prepared to marvel at all of my interview insights. Throughout all of my experiences, I have realized that, in the end, all that counts is you and your families' happiness. No matter how well-paying or popular the job may be, without happiness, you have nothing. So look within yourself before you leap into any situation. Make sure that there is a variety of aspects about the position that thrill you. No one knows you better than you know yourself. Ask questions and be demanding of the answers that you seek. In the end, the entire process affects you and your family, so do not make any rash decisions. Be yourself. Do not put on a front that you are going to have to live up to for the rest of your career.

If there is one thing that I have learned, it is that money is not worth it all the time. It is not worth the title or the high-paying salary, if you are unhappy at the end of the day. This book prepares you with questions that are necessary for your well-being.

Index